ROCHESTER HHUNTS
A Ghost Hunter's Guide

Dwayne Claud

Schiffer Publishing Ltd

4880 Lower Valley Road, Atglen, Pennsylvania 19310

Schiffer Books are available at special discounts for bulk purchases for sales promotions or premiums. Special editions, including personalized covers, corporate imprints, and excerpts can be created in large quantities for special needs. For more information contact the publisher:

Schiffer Publishing Ltd.
4880 Lower Valley Road
Atglen, PA 19310
Phone: (610) 593-1777; Fax: (610) 593-2002
E-mail: Info@schifferbooks.com

For the largest selection of fine reference books on this and related subjects, please visit our web site at **www.schifferbooks.com**

We are always looking for people to write books on new and related subjects. If you have an idea for a book please contact us at the above address.

This book may be purchased from the publisher. Include $5.00 for shipping. Please try your bookstore first. You may write for a free catalog.

In Europe, Schiffer books are distributed by:
Bushwood Books
6 Marksbury Ave.
Kew Gardens
Surrey TW9 4JF England
Phone: 44 (0) 20 8392-8585; Fax: 44 (0) 20 8392-9876
E-mail: info@bushwoodbooks.co.uk
Website: www.bushwoodbooks.co.uk
Free postage in the U.K., Europe; air mail at cost.

Copyright © 2009 by Dwayne Claud
Library of Congress Control Number: 2008939984

Designed by Stephanie Daugherty
Type set in Empire BT/Futura LtCn BT/New Baskerville BT

ISBN: 978-0-7643-3208-1
Printed in the United States of America

DEDICATION

This book is dedicated to my wife, Sarah, and my three children who stuck with me through all the research and late nights of writing. It is also dedicated to all the departed spirits whose stories can finally be told.

AUTHOR'S NOTE

It's been a number of years since I initially became interested in the paranormal. When it first happened, it was indeed the stuff movies were made of—by my being plunged into it with a demonic experience. It was an encounter that changed my life and the lives of those around me. I experienced things that I was taught could never happen. It challenged my beliefs. It challenged my faith. It opened my eyes to all of possibilities that are in this world beyond our five senses and into another realm of existence.

As I continue on this journey, I've come to realize that there are no "true experts" in the field of the paranormal, whether the area of interest be UFOs, cryptozoology, or ghosts—no matter who they are. Certainly there are some who have a greater amount of experience than others, but ghosts, in general, are just as mysterious to us today as they were before the days of Christ. The paranormal groups investigating the unknown in the Rochester area and beyond are to be applauded. Remember, no matter your background, bring it because you can make a difference. After all, Einstein began as a janitor and look at the changes he brought to humanity. You can do the same.

CONTENTS

FOREWORD

I n all the many years that I've led tour groups of people along the streets of Mt. Hope Cemetery and the sidewalks of Irondequoit, I've learned that everyone has a story to tell and that every street has a secret it hides. Rochester, New York, is no different than any other city across the nation. She, too, has had her share of booming successes—from growing and expanding during the early pioneer days and being built on the strength of the Erie Canal, to the entrepreneur genius of George Eastman, founder of Kodak. She's had her challenges, though, surviving the Great Depression, fires that destroyed blocks of city buildings, and a pandemic that killed thousands over the course of just a few weeks. Remaining are spirits, waiting for their stories to be heard.

Even though the world we live in today is a world of skepticism, open up your mind to the possibilities. Remember, humanity once thought that the world was flat, until science was finally able to prove otherwise. Couldn't that also be true of the spirit realm? I'd like to encourage you to lay aside the idea that ghostly presences from the past are simply remnants from a long past time of superstition, and for a moment, consider the phantom history of Rochester.

The idea that some of those individuals who first came to Rochester so many years ago had the drive to tame a frontier, to control the land, and to build empires may still remain. The price that they all paid was steeped in their sweat and blood, while many had their lives taken before their time. Consider for a moment that there may still remain some holding onto their passion and ambition beyond death itself; others remaining deeply attached to their family or property and choosing to remain as a ghostly memory from the past.

Haunted Rochester: A Ghost Hunter's Guide is a wonderful collection of spirited stories and tales sharing some of Rochester's most famous and infamous hauntings—from the legend of the White Lady of Durand Eastman Park and the spirit of Sam Patch, to personal stories and experiences, some funny and others terrifying. If you choose to believe or not, the decision is yours. But should you meet a traveler along your journey, only to discover that they've disappeared once you've turned to talk to them, consider the message they may be trying to share with you about the phantom history of Rochester.

Ralph Esposito
Author, *Ghosts of Old Rochesterville*
www.reparanormal.com

INTRODUCTION

A Little Ghost Hunting History...

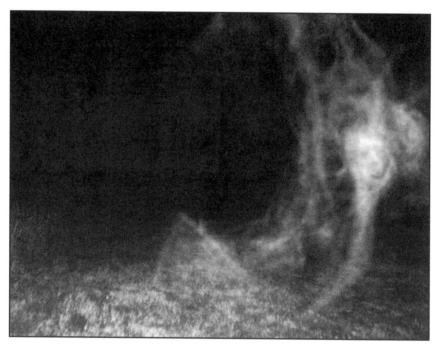

The fascination with life beyond death is one that is as old as humanity itself. The earliest recorded investigation of a haunted house was in 100 A.D. in Athens Greece by a philosopher named Athenodorus. In the book, *Appearances of the Dead: A Cultural History of Ghosts* by R.C. Fiucane, the author recounts a story recorded by a gentleman named Pliny the Younger about how the home was haunted by the ghost of an emaciated looking gentleman. The spectre would rattle his chains at night bringing disease and death to those who lived in the home. Philosopher Athenodorus purchased the Athens home and at first tried to ignore the spectre, until one day he followed it to where it disappeared in the garden. Athenodorus contacted local officials who came to the home and dug in the area where the spectre had vanished to find his bones. Once a proper burial was conducted, the haunting ceased. Is this a true account or just a story that has grown through the ages? Even if it is just folklore or an urban legend from a time long ago, accounts like these have some basis in truth and are found in every culture around the world.

In 1862, the Ghost Club was formed in London, England. It was a group of individuals dedicated to determining if there was life after death by investigating so-called spiritual haunting through the use of nineteenth-century science. Of the members, perhaps the most famous were Sir Charles Dickens and famed magician Harry Price. Around the same time, Stanly Hall, who was considered an American philosopher and also founder of the American Psychological Association, began a collaboration with other individuals in the United States and England to form the Society for Psychical Research in order to collect data and potential evidence relating to haunted houses, apparitions, ghosts, and other unexplained spiritual phenomenon.

By the 1950s and 60s, independent researchers began to become active in the field. German researcher Hans Holzer and Americans investigators Ed and Lorraine Warren became leaders in the field. Today more than 300 paranormal research teams are active across the United States alone. Television programs such as the Sci Fi Channel's *Ghost Hunters* and A&E's *Paranormal State* have drawn more interest into the field. More individuals become interested daily with more groups forming every week coming from every background imaginable. What makes the field of paranormal research so phenomenal is the vast backgrounds that researchers are coming from. The wide range of lifetime experiences provides a multitude of different perspectives for questions no one person has the answers to, and may never.

Time to Gear Up...

Grab your gear and head out for a fun and exciting journey into the world of paranormal investigation. There's no place better to start your experiences than in Rochester, New York. But wait, you don't know what equipment you need? Not a problem whatsoever because you have a lot of the tools that you need right at home. Come on, let's go rummage through the closet and see what we can find!

Regardless of what an individual may see on television, investigators don't need all of the fancy gizmos and gadgets that they see on television or read about in books. In fact, Vince Wilson, author of *Ghost Science*, discovered in his research that the use of much of this equipment didn't exist before 1984. Before that time, investigators would never have thought of taking EMF readings, looking for temperature variations, or using night vision goggles, among other pieces of equipment.

Be skeptical! What you see may not be what it truly *is*.

Any good researcher on their first investigation should go with an open mind. They may find something, or they may not. It's important to be open to all the possibilities while still keeping a healthy balance of skepticism. Take your time, make certain you have permission to be on the premises, and be courteous to property owners and spirits alike.

When preparing for the field, consider bringing with you some of these basic pieces of equipment for your adventure:

1. **Camera:** The type of camera that the investigator uses is completely up to their own preference—whether it be film or digital. If you choose to use a film camera, 35mm film should be the film of choice with a film speed of 400 ASL or higher. But there have also been some extraordinary photographs taken with disposable 35mm cameras as well. If digital is your choice, then look for a camera that delivers 6 mega pixels or greater. The greater the resolution there is, the less chance there is for false positives, so be certain to take your photographs with the highest possible resolution setting. Many of the new SONY Cybershot cameras come with a special "night vision" feature so that a photographic flash need not be used and pictures can be taken in the dark. Photographic evidence can many times capture what the eye can not see because the object moves too fast or is operating on a different wavelength of light—a wavelength not visible to the naked eye. All cameras take photographs in a much wider range of wavelengths of light then what the eye can see.

The next opportunity you have, try and take a photograph of infrared light to prove this to yourself. Simply take a remote control for your television, while holding one of the buttons down take a picture of the little bulb at the end. When you look at the picture, you will see the red light glowing, but you didn't see that with your eyes. That is a photograph on the infrared spectrum.

Now there are advantages and disadvantages to each style of camera, so it's really up to the investigator which factors are most important to them. Film cameras provide a negative of any photograph taken. If any evidence is gathered, there is hard proof of it, but there can also be development errors; so beware. Digital cameras give instant gratification whether or not any phenomenon is captured, but digital images can be easily altered so evidence may always be in question. And one of the most important factors is the economical factor of digital cameras. Sometimes thousands of photographs can be taken with no unexplained images...that's a lot of dollars processing blank film. Many investigators suggest asking to take the spirit's photograph. It would seem that being polite with the dead has its advantages, too.

2. **Audio recorder:** As much audio as you record, you will have to listen to, but some of the most compelling evidence is in the form of electronic voice phenomenon or EVP. There is nothing more intriguing then being in a room alone. Asking questions. And when you go back to listen to the recording, hearing another voice respond to your questions. There is a wide variety of opinions as to the best type of audio recorder to use, digital or analog. The key with either recorder is to record on the highest quality available. Many times this will use up space on the digital recorder or on the analog tape much quicker, but it also reduces the extra noise and provides for a much cleaner recording. A clean recording is always the key, so it's important to use an omnidirectional external microphone when attempting to capture EVP. This moves the recording microphone out away from the box and away from the motor noise itself, thereby reducing noise once again. Other techniques that are also used include placing the recorder and microphone down while attempting EVP, or even mounting the microphone on the end of a long wooden dowel, wrapping the cord around the dowel to reduce the noise of the microphone or cord moving.

When you ask questions, speak loudly. Don't whisper. Whispers can be mistaken for EVP upon review, and after each question, pause for the response. Each session should be more than thirty minutes at a time. After that time span, go back and listen for responses. If there are none, you can move on to another room. But if there is a response, you may have an opportunity to adjust your questions to gather more information. As you listen for possible responses, the researcher should listen through a set of headphones and listen for even the smallest whisper, or for voices speaking over top of others. You will be surprised with what you may find.

3. **Video recorder:** Video recorders are unique in that you can capture moving objects that can't be seen with the naked eye. The problem is that it takes your focus away from what is going on around you and leads that focus into the viewfinder. If you decide that video is a medium that's important to the investigation, choose a Sony brand video recorder. These recorders come with the special "night shot" feature which allows for recording in darkness. It uses an infrared light to light the area being recorded which dramatically reduces any flash back or false positives. IR boosters are also available to increase the amount of lit field. When the footage is reviewed for potential evidence, listen to the audio at the same time through headphones. Some of the best EVPs are captured using video recorders because of the high recording quality of the audio. Unfortunately, many times these EVPs are missed because individuals are too focused on the picture and are ignoring the sound. It's not usual to hear an EVP that corresponds with a unexplained phenomenon on the screen.

4. **Notebook:** It's important to carry a small notebook along with a pen or pencil. It can be used to record any feelings that you have and to make notes about the different areas you explore as well as certain things to remember when reviewing the evidence. (It comes in real handy to use for *Tic Tac Toe* as well while waiting in the dark for something to happen.)

5. **Flashlight:** A flashlight is the investigator's best friend in the field. Remember, ghosts can't hurt you, but you can break your neck on something you don't see in the darkness. Avoid the bright white flashlights. They cause night blindness and can cause lens flare and reflection. Instead, look for an LED light with either a red or green cast. Green should be the first choice, because it is very difficult to see in infrared and most cameras won't capture its reflection.

Now if you'd like to go old school with your paranormal investigation, here's a few other items that you could consider adding to your tool kit:

1. **Compass:** Compasses are the low tech version of instruments known as EMF or electromagnetic field detectors. These instruments read variations in the electromagnetic field in the environment. It's believed that spirits are composed entirely of energy. When there is paranormal activity in the area, there are changes in the magnetic and electric fields in the environment. A compass can be used to detect changes in magnetic fields in an environment. Spiritual activity in a room can attract the north end of the needle. It will then follow the movement of the spirit in the room, sometimes moving as much as ten to fifteen degrees from the normal North reading. When this occurs, investigators should point their camera in the direction of the disturbance and take a picture. Many times, some very unique photographs can be captured by noticing these small variations.

2. **Pendulum:** A pendulum is a dowsing tool that can be used to detect spiritual energy and on some level communicate with the spirit. A simple pendulum consists of a heavy weight at the end of a string or light chain. The weight can be a crystal, rock, or some have even been wood bobbers. The investigator simply holds the string or chain between their thumb and pointer finger, and while the weight hangs, they begin to ask questions. First establishing what a "yes" response is and then what a "no" response is. Each swing is different but the investigator needs to be careful to hold their arm completely still as to not influence the movements of the pendulum itself. This can be accomplished by resting the arm on a table or other sturdy device.

3. **Dowsing rods:** There are two types of dowsing rods that individuals can use. The first is in the shape of a "y" which is the traditional rod used to dowse for water. The other are in the shape of an "L" which are more commonly used for spiritual dowsing. The L-shaped rods, are usually made of brass or copper and have a handle which allows the rods to swing freely. Investigators hold a rod in each hand, level and with a gentle grip, asking simple *yes* or *no* questions. As with the pendulum, they would establish what a "yes" response would be and then what a "no" response would be. Commonly, the rods cross for one and separate for the other. When asked, they will

point to the spirit in the room and as the investigator walks close, will cross or open wide depending upon your response for "yes."

4. **Your own senses:** Trust yourself. Everyone has a sixth sense. Pay attention to it. There are a few ways that ghosts communicate at a telepathic level. They can verbalize words through thoughts. Just like a radio wave, they send out the thought and the intuitive part of your brain can "hear" it. It is a very primitive form of telepathy, but yes, you have it. We all do, most of us just never use it. The challenge with this form of communication is that it is difficult to determine what is imagination, your own thoughts, or the actual spirit's words. Quite honestly, the spirit's voice and thoughts are vastly different from your own, so it's not as difficult to distinguish once you recognize the difference. Another way that they may communicate is by sending waves of pictures into your consciousness. Flashes of places, people, and events may involuntarily dance into your thoughts. Don't ignore these, trust your sixth sense. These images may hold clues as to what the spirit wants from you or to tell you. They are on this realm for a reason, usually to right a wrong that occurred in life; they are trying to help you to understand what they need to say. Thirdly, communication can occur with intense sensations. They can impress physical sensation onto you possibly explaining what caused their death. This can be unpleasant, but not intolerable. You may just feel a tingling or light pain where the ghost incurred injury in life.

Now that you have your tools, you're ready to hit the field ghost hunting. Bringing just these few tools with you will help you to capture some amazing things that under normal circumstances would go unseen or unheard normally. Enter this world with an open mind, for as Hamlet said, "there are more things in Heaven and Earth Horatio than are dreamt of in your philosophies." Laugh and have fun while you explore some of these locations because the more positive energy and respect you place into your adventure, the more of that same spiritual energy you will receive in response. The spirits can feel your enthusiasm and are more likely to come out when you are being positive and welcoming.

1

WELCOME TO ROCHESTER, NEW YORK

There is a city that hides behind the corporate veils of companies such as Kodak, Bausch and Lomb, and Xerox. It's a city that is known as Rochester. Paranormal activity has long been a mainstay of this small Western New York community. According to Mason Winfield, its reputation for occult activity was once so strong that it was known as the "City of 1,000 Ghosts." (Winfield, 2003,78) Anyone who studies the Spiritualist movement knows that it began with two sisters in Hydesville, New York. John and Margaret Fox were devout Methodists living in Hydesville, New York in 1848 when the first events took place. Their four adult children had long since moved away and started families of their own, leaving the youngest daughters Margaretta and Catherine (Maggie and Kate), in their small home. One night in March, the family was asleep when strange noises abruptly startled them awake. Reportedly, a variety of bangs, raps, and similar sounds kept the Fox family up that night, and every night for the rest of the week. They searched for, but could not find, a source for the mysterious sounds. It was on March 31, the date often recognized as the birth of Spiritualism, when Kate, the younger of the two girls, decided to try and discover what was causing the rapping. She asked the noise to rap ten times. It did. Kate's questions became more complicated, querying as to the ages of the six Fox children, among other things, and each time the tapping responded perfectly. (Keene,2007) Through a series of question and answer sessions with the source, Kate discovered that the noise was that of a spirit peddler who'd been murdered and buried in the basement of the Fox house some years past. The spiritual communication was given validity when human remains were reportedly unearthed beneath the floor of the small cottage. As word of the occurrences spread, the girls gained fame for their discovery of what would set off a veritable wildfire of Spiritualist activity. The sisters conducted many sessions outside of their own home as well, including a session in the Hyde House, perhaps better known as the Octagon House, that is now located at the Genesee Country Village in Mumford, New York. In April 1848, news of the now locally famous "Hydesville Rappings" reached the ears of Leah Fox Fish, Maggie and Kate's older sister. Middle-aged Leah lived with her adolescent daughter in nearby Rochester, New York. Her husband had abandoned her and her daughter, so when Mrs. Fish saw the opportunity to capitalize on the fame of her younger sisters, she decided to seize it. Kate had to move to her brother's house in Auburn, New York, while Margaret took refuge at her sister Leah's house on Plymouth Avenue in Rochester. Raps broke out at both places, indicating that it was the young girls who were supplying the necessary, vital energy for spirit to manifest as it did. The raps were particularly violent in Leah's house. The violent disturbances continued in Leah's house until a friend named Isaac Post remembered that the girls' brother, David, had once conversed with the Hydesville spirits using the alphabet. As an experiment, they tried this method again with the following results:

"Dear Friends, you must proclaim this truth to the world. This is the dawning of a new era; you must not try to conceal it any longer. When you do your duty God will protect you and good spirits will watch over you."

From that time onward, the communications poured forth and the manifestations were orderly and nonviolent in nature. The successful relaying of the above message apparently released the frustration and urgency on the part of spirit, thereby allowing more orderly and cohesive communication. Imagine, if you can, the sense of release you would feel if, after trying so very hard to convey a message to someone without success, you were suddenly able to do so. This is exactly what spirit experienced during this period. Although later on, the Fox Sisters would undergo considerable heat with allegations of fraud and hoax, these allegations would never be proven beyond a shadow of a doubt. The commercial successes this family had lead to a much more important element, a way of believing in life after death, modern Spiritualism. Spiritualism is a philosophy: it studies the laws of nature on both the seen and unseen sides of life and bases its conclusions upon present observed facts. It strives to understand the relationship between the physical, spiritual, and mental laws of nature that God has put into place. In 1856, Rochester became the home to one of the first Spiritualist Churches in the country built across the street from the home of Leah Fox, where a memorial plaque remains today. (Keene, 2007) Spiritualism has evolved much since those first days when the physical phenomenon were used to "wow them in the aisles" to build a basis for the faith. Today, more emphasis has been placed on mental mediumship and healing. The faith continues to grow with Churches across the world, and will remain alive and well, as long as there is a curiosity in life after death.

2

PRAISE THE "SPIRIT"

The word "haunted" invokes fear into people. Their hearts pound. Their palms drip with sweat—waiting for things in the darkness to come and get them. The truth is that it's very unusual to have "anything" get you in the dark, unless it's a member of the family trying to scare you. Places that have unexplained paranormal activity are not always dark corners and places of ruin. Many are just the opposite.

Churches and places of worship are not often thought of as places of paranormal activity but they are. The Spiritualist religion celebrated union with the spirit and praised life after death just as many other religions do. In these places, individuals celebrate the spirit and belief in a higher power. They build a community of family and friends sharing their belief and faith. The next service you attend, open yourself up to the positive energy and feel loved ones by your side.

Plymouth Spiritualist Church
29 Vick Park A
Rochester, New York
www.plymouthspiritualistchurch.org

The Plymouth Spiritualist Church in Rochester is known as the "mother church of modern Spiritualism." Originally located at the corner of Troupe and Plymouth Street, the church was built in 1856. It remained at this location until March of 2002, when it was moved to the current location.

A visitation to a Spiritualist service is truly a unique experience where everyone is welcome. It's a mix of science and religion where they welcome the spirit while trying to prove its existence through communication between the worlds. Like any other religious service, there is generally a sharing of the word of God and singing of songs. What you won't find at many other religious services outside of Spiritualism are opportunities for physical, emotional, and spiritual healing by one of the church's many practitioners, or the opportunity to participate in a gallery reading by a guest medium. It's during this time that messages of inspiration from departed loved ones are given to the congregation—messages that intend to affirm love and joy while helping them through whatever personal circumstance occurring for them at this time in their life.

The experience at the Plymouth Spiritualist Church or any Spiritualist church is one that draws in the spirit with its joy and faith. Experiments have been done in many Spiritualist churches where audio recordings were made during services or "calls to spirit" only to hear responses from beyond. Photographs have been taken during these same sessions only to reveal spirit orbs present. Proof from beyond the grave that our loved ones still come when we need to them to help, heal and guide us.

Our Lady of Victory Church
210 Pleasant Street
Rochester, New York

As part of the Rochester Catholic Diocese, the Our Lady of Victory Church was built in 1864 on Pleasant Street. As was common in those times, each nationality had their own church in Rochester even though they might all have been Catholic. Our Lady of Victory was known as the "little French church" in Rochester. Some historical accounts show that prior to this land being used as a church, it is was used as a school for the Diocese, known as the Sacred Heart—a school where they would instruct individuals for the nunnery and priesthood. The Sacred Heart wasn't long for this location before moving elsewhere in Rochester to make room for public religious services.

It's often found that places of great religious faith draw spirits from beyond, and Out Lady of Victory is no different. According to an October 1993 article in the *Rochester Democrat and Chronicle*, it's not uncommon for those that live around the Pleasant Street church to see unexplained phenomenon roaming its grounds. Eye witnesses have reported ghostly figures that appear in a small courtyard adjacent to the church. They seem to appear quite regularly during times that the flowers are in bloom and the gardens are lush, congregating around the statue of the Virgin Mary. To many they are a joyous gathering of spirits that bring forth feelings of love and acceptance.

Childtime Learning Center
55 Hoover Drive
Greece, New York

Located at the corner of Ridge Road and Hoover Drive in Greece is the Childtime Learning Center inside a once prosperous church. Why would a church contain spirits? Churches are places of great spiritual energy. Individuals gather together in one place to build their faith and develop camaraderie. They share prayer and sing songs of worship. Churches are homes of joyous occasions such as baptisms and marriages and also that of mourning when people have passed. The church becomes a building of great spiritual power, power that builds and builds and never has a release, so it's not uncommon for spiritual visitors to come through or even to have residual haunting appear from the great energy gathered.

Today, the church on Hoover Drive now serves as a Childtime Learning Center. According to some of their employees, both current and former, spirits still roam the halls of this building. Teachers tell of a mysterious presence they experienced in the classroom one day. They described it as a huge black mass that was wide enough to fill the entire doorway in the upstairs classroom. Before they knew it, a row of cubbies tumbled and the mass went right through one of the teachers. Later that same night, after the children had gone home, the trash lids in the main room flew across the classroom with no one visibly in the room to toss them. The activity though hasn't been limited to times when the children were absent. There have been reports of water turning on and off during children's nap times with the sounds of footsteps walking the floor above. The building has secured entry into it, so no one could sneak in. The building was empty except for those who were in the classroom.

Lisa Steinmetz, a former employee, sat one day working on lesson plans during nap time, only to hear whispers coming from the empty bathroom. Thinking one of the children had woken, she went to the bathroom only to find it empty, but the whispering continued. She was only there a moment when she felt someone lean over her shoulder to whisper in her ear, "Lisa." She turned to find no one there. Thinking it was just her imagination, she returned to work and then caught, out of the corner of her eye, a dark shadow darting across the doorway into the hall. Thinking it was her supervisor, Lisa went to talk to her only to find her supervisor in her office behind a closed door.

One of Childtime's past directors, Mrs. Sara, shared that is wasn't uncommon to hear the sound of a crying baby when the building was empty, and that there was also the spirit of a young girl that she would see in the vestibule—a young girl that would dance across the stage area, and would also come down into the classroom locale. She never described what she was wearing but apparently this young spirit felt at home in this place of worship, among the children.

3

"REST" IN PEACE

W hat lies beneath the ground under scattered stones of marble are but mere husks. They are only a remnant of what we once were, an empty shell without a soul. A soul that has left the body since it died. So, if all that riddles the landscape of a graveyard are but empty husks of those forgotten, why would a cemetery be haunted?

There are many things that walk among among the stones once the moon rises. Consider this: the power of faith. If you had faith in the idea that once you died, your soul went to Heaven. What could happen if all you believed was that your body would lie in the ground after death and there was no where to go afterwards? Cemeteries are considered a final resting place. What if your grave were disturbed or moved? Perhaps your soul would walk among the stones. If a place of worship and its congregation can generate such positive power through faith and prayer to bring angels, what could a place of mourning and sorrow attract? There are many things that can walk among the stones. Beware, because not all spirits are ready to rest and some may have never lived at all.

Mount Hope Cemetery
791 Mount Hope Avenue
Rochester, New York
www.fomh.org

A visit to Rochester isn't complete for the avid ghost hunter without an expedition to the famous Mount Hope Cemetery. The cemetery opened in 1867, and is the oldest municipal cemetery in the United States. The cemetery itself covers over 196 acres with more than fourteen miles of roads winding through the breathtaking grounds. For then, and even now, the size of Mount Hope was much larger than any other cemetery in the region. This was in part due to a small pox outbreak which had filled many of the local area cemeteries during that time. Mount Hope was intended to not only receive new burials, but also to safely receive the removals from smaller, over-filled cemeteries in the region. As Rochester grew, additional land was required from these small cemeteries for the construction of schools and hospitals. The older burials were placed in mass graves within Mount Hope, with newer burials in individual plots, sometimes with headstones. Currently there are over 350,000 graves including such notables as Frederick Douglas and Susan B. Anthony.

The Mount Hope Cemetery is both beautiful and awe-inspiring during the day, but beware if you become locked inside the cemetery at night. Don't trust your eyes or your senses too much because what you think you see, you may not. Stories have been shared by individuals who have had the misfortune of being trapped. Shadowy figures that you may see walking among the tombstones may not be the ghosts the young paranormal investigator hopes they are.

One gentleman tells of a night he became locked behind the gates of Mount Hope. As he was walking towards the gate house, he saw dark-hooded figures moving among the headstones with what appeared to be a ball of light suspended in the air next to them. Not believing his eyes, he moved closer to the dark figures, only to find out that what he was seeing were indeed dark-hooded individuals. But instead of a ball of light floating beside them, they were carrying torches and performing some ritual. He went unnoticed, or did he?

October is always an interesting time around Mount Hope Cemetery. Along the sidewalk are lit candle luminaries that

05/26/2007

Hovering above this forgotten gravestone is what appears to be a mist and spirit orb.
Photograph by Lisa Carpenter of Hamlin, New York.

flicker in the darkness as the Rochester Candlelight Ghost Walks organization lead people around the perimeter of the cemetery, telling tales of the burial ground from both a historical and ghostly perspective. One favorite story presenter, Ralph Esposito, likes to tell of the full-moon night when the staff was closing the doors of a local restaurant and bar across the street from the main entrance to the cemetery. He relates how the closing staff of the Distillery glanced across the street to see a glowing ball behind the gates. They didn't think much more about it, until one of them glanced back over to see the ball becoming bigger as it traveled towards the gate and then became fiery in nature. It passed through the bars of the main gate and then "poof!" It vanished. Could this have been one of the ghostly residents of the cemetery? Perhaps, the fiery ball was from one of the rituals conducted in the cemetery, or the spirits of the alcohol they consumed that made their presence known.

05/26/2007

The mist looks very much like a hooded figure.
Photograph by Lisa Carpenter of Hamlin, New York.

One of the other presenters, Jenni Oneski, who is also director of the East Ghost Paranormal Society, shares her experience of being locked in the cemetery one night after dark. With the gates locked, Oneski looked around for someone to assist her when she noticed someone actually jogging down one of the roads in the cemetery. As she approached him, the EMF meter she had been carrying with her went off and the jogger disappeared into thin air. (Oneski, 2005) Could this man have been so entwined in his own health that he continues to jog even after his own death, or could it have been a residual haunting where an individual relived one event over and over so many times that their energy left a permanent imprint?

These are just a couple of the wonderful stories told by this group of investigators about Mount Hope Cemetery. A walk with these ghost hunters is both an enlightening and

In the early twilight hours, a spirit finds a resting place.
Photograph by Lisa Carpenter of Hamlin, New York.

entertaining experience. Regardless, even a walk alone in the cemetery will be one to open up your eyes to the spirit world. Just be wary—do not become stranded inside until morning.

Holy Sepulchre Cemetery
2461 Lake Avenue
Greece, New York
www.holysepulchre.org

The first Catholic Parish came to Rochester in 1823. This downtown church had a small gravesite next to it, which it quickly outgrew, forcing individuals to purchase gravesites in "common" or multi-denominational cemeteries. In 1839, a second Catholic Cemetery was opened that encompassed twenty-one acres. Its purpose was to serve the Irish Catholic Community. At the time, four German Catholic Churches began to serve the Rochester area, each with their own gravesites.

This would change in 1871, when Rochester's first Bishop began at the Rochester Diocese. Bishop McQuaid felt that it was inappropriate and impractical to have so many Catholic gravesites in one region so, farmland was purchased to create the Holy Sepulchre Cemetery. It's estimated that over 5,000 bodies were moved from their original resting places and re-interred into this cemetery with the latest transfer in the 1950s. Today, the cemetery spans 332 acres and is perhaps one of the most active cemeteries in Greece, but it was in August of 1909 that things changed for this peaceful cemetery in Greece, New York.

Young Anna Schumadher had made it a routine to visit the graves at Holy Sepulchre. Perhaps an unusual place for a seventeen-year-old girl, but these visits were actual errands of love. She would frequently visit the gravesites of her father and sister who were buried there. She was known in the community for decorating their memorials with fresh flowers. According to an article in the *New York Times* dated August 10, 1909, Anna was reported missing after her daily visit on August 8, 1909, when she failed to return back home. Her family searched the cemetery to no avail, and when she did not return, they then notified the police department. It was on the morning of August 9th that the police department began their search. They soon found marks of a struggle and signs of something being dragged. Law enforcement followed the trail that lead to a depression behind some undergrowth. It was there that they found sticking out from the loose earth, pieces of white clothing which lead them to begin to dig to find her body. Her body crumbled up into a fetal position with her knees pulled into her chest, lying face down with her face resting in the hat she had worn. In the hat were Anna's torn undergarments. It was apparent the struggled Anna had put up a struggle as there were bruises over her entire body, as well as scratches and blood. Anna had been strangled. A spade was later found covered in dried blood which was used to bury her. One week later, Anna's killer turned himself in, explaining that the two had been flirting for a few days. But when he tried to kiss her on that fatal day, she backed away and things went too far. Since that time, individuals who have visited the cemetery tell of a gray lady that roams the roads within Holy Sepulchre Cemetery. A gray lady is a woman who died by the hands of her lover and forever walks the place where she died looking for him. Could the gray lady of Holy Sepulchre be Anna or could it be someone else—like a victim of Jack The Ripper.

Many don't realize that Holy Sepulchre Cemetery is the resting place of the only American suspect in the Jack The Ripper killings, Dr. Francis Tumuelty. Tumuelty was known for his shady medical practices, con jobs, perverse behavior, and hatred of women. The doctor was in Whitechapel at the time of the Ripper murders. He had motive and anatomical knowledge. The only confirmed victim of the "doctor," whose medical degree is highly questionable, is a Canadian who died from one of Tumuelty's procedures. Tumuelty fled Canada back to his hometown of Rochester to escape the charges. He similarly fled England after being arrested for a misdemeanor charge. The Ripper murders ceased immediately upon him fleeing the country. English authorities were unable to extradite him once he'd returned to America.

In October of 2005, a local Rochester radio station took it upon themselves to "reach out beyond the grave" to Jack The Ripper as part of a radio stunt for Halloween. They sent a young intern out to the cemetery with a Ouija Board. While he was there, he could swear that he heard the sounds of babies crying. But he was in a cemetery before the crack of dawn, so that couldn't be possible. He put that thought out of his mind and attempted to communicate with Tumuelty. He tried for quite sometime, but was unsuccessful. The intern placed the Ouija Board under his arm and headed for this car. At first, his car didn't want to start. It just turned over and over. Dawn was being to break, so the fear of getting stuck in a cemetery wasn't quite as scary. He took a deep breath and tried one more

Legend has it that the ashes of Jack The Ripper are placed in the urn at the top of the monument because they were too evil to bury.
Photograph by Stacie Barry, Western New York Paranormal.

time; this time the car started and he began his way back to the radio station. It was only a few miles from the cemetery when it happened.

A deer jumped in front of him out of nowhere. Coincidence? Well, over the next several weeks, this gentleman had a severe run of bad luck, and accidents. It was then that a psychic was brought in who had recently dealt with a terrible haunting that had happened on the Alfred State Campus. The psychic sensed an entity had attached itself to him, one of great dark power. After several attempts to cleanse this individual, the entity returned to where it came from and the intern returned to a normal life.

But what of the sounds of babies crying in the cemetery? As it turns out, there have been many reports of the sounds of infants crying the cemetery late at night, ghostly cries for help in the darkness. It was in 1908 that the bodies of two new born infants were found in the cemetery. According to the May 30, 1908 edition of the *Democrat and Chronicle*, it was on the morning of May 29, 1908, when two women walking through the cemetery stumbled across a small basket. In the basket was a tiny object wrapped in red linen partially covered by fallen leaves. They were shocked upon moving the linen to find the bodies of two young newborns, a set of twins. There was one boy and one girl. It was never determined who the children were, but an autopsy showed that these infants were smothered to death. Now, it's perhaps the spirits of these two innocent souls that cry for help in the darkness at the corner of sections G and H at Holy Sepulchre Cemetery.

Mount Pleasant Cemetery
Lakeville Road (Route 20A)
Geneseo, New York

There is a small cemetery on top of a knoll overlooking the beautiful Genesee Valley. Before construction of interstate 390, many people would likely have passed by this resting ground with little notice—unless you were a traveler sightseeing the breathtaking Conesus Lake. The Mount Pleasant Cemetery, established in 1823, is about a thirty-minute drive south of Rochester, located just off the Geneseo exit of Route 390, and is a restful internment place—be it day or night. The cemetery itself is filled with over a thousand souls, many of which date back to the revolutionary war. But as visitors enter the cemetery gates, they may just be greeted by the spirit of a young girl. No one is certain of her name or why she remains there, but she is anxious to be heard. She is around the age of six, and if a hand is placed down for her to hold, you just may feel her icy touch as she takes your hand.

One of the first investigations Drew Beeman of the Twin Tiers Paranormal Group conducted was at the Mount Pleasant Cemetery. He had always had an interest in what was on "the Other Side," if there really *was* an other side. He took it upon himself to learn more by attending a local conference on the paranormal. This is where he gained his first piece of ghost hunting equipment, a small RCA digital recorder. It wasn't anything special; it wasn't high-tech—it was simply a digital recorder that cost $19.95 and could be purchased at any local Wal-Mart. What made the recorder special to him, though, was that it was given to him by Todd Bates, a leading researcher in Electronic Voice Phenomenon. Little did Beeman know, this gift would be his first tool to give him a glimpse into the unknown.

Beeman was a local Geneseo resident. He thought it would be fun to investigate some of the local haunts. Although never hearing a ghost story about Mount Pleasant, he thought it would be fun and interesting to investigate a cemetery anyway. On a cool May evening, Beeman with two other investigators, walked into the cemetery looking for signs of the paranormal. Although only there for about an hour, nothing spectacular occurred. Nothing jumped out to say, "Boo!" It was, in a way, a bit disappointing, because it wasn't what he expected to happen on a ghost hunt. It was when he went back and began to listen to the recordings he

"Hello?"

had taken with that same small recorder that was given to him that he changed his mind.

They hadn't been in the graveyard for two minutes when a voice was calling to them from the darkness, "Hello?" It was the voice of a young girl, who sounded around the age of six. It was a recording caught not only on one recorder, but on two—simultaneously. A young girl just looking for someone to hold her hand in the darkness, and just one of the entities that you will meet at Mount Pleasant.

It has been said by passersby of this place that a woman wearing dark clothes stands vigilant towards the back of the cemetery, an older woman who pays respect to a departed husband. She is quite peaceful and silent. She has been described as short in stature, with a round, soft face. Her eyes are kind, and she has short, white hair… and although mourning, still has a welcoming smile. This widow carries a single red rose for her husband, and when she is acknowledged for paying her respects, she fades away into the darkness.

Daylight or night, it doesn't seem to affect the activity at Mount Pleasant. Those active there are simply spirits seeking to be noticed. The increased traffic activity of Interstate 390 has perhaps raised their energy levels enough to call for the attention, or maybe it has been so long since they have had regular visitors that they have decided to beckon friendly faces in for a visit.

West Middlebury Cemetery
4949 West Middlebury Road
West Middlebury, New York

The West Middlebury Cemetery is one of Wyoming County's oldest and most spiritually active cemeteries. It's located approximately an hour south of Rochester, just minutes from the Rolling Hills Country Mall. This cemetery, with just about 100 cemetery plots and numerous unmarked graves, can be dated to the late 1700s—the very beginning of settlement in the region. The cemetery has very little use now.

Western New York Paranormal discovered during their investigations that there is a caretaker spirit that roams the grounds. Her name is Mary-Mary Chaddock to be precise. It was initially the team sensitive, Sarah Claud, who discovered the existence of the spirit. During an investigation of the cemetery, she drew Sarah to a large pillar-shaped stone that stood at the back of the cemetery. At the stone, an incredible EVP was captured on an audio recording. Simultaneously, another team member was physically halted by a spirit there. It was later that night, during the investigation, that an image was captured on infrared video. It was the image of a ghostly white figure pacing in front of the large stone pillar—the image of a woman. The name on the stone was "Mary" which was spoken by the team sensitive before another investigator was able to confirm the writing on the stone.

Over the next few months, the team conducted some extensive research into the history of the cemetery and region, more specifically into the entity claiming to be "Mary." Initially, they had trouble finding the connection, but the information that Mary was imparting to the sensitive through various contacts began to collaborate with historical records—once they realized that "Mary" was a nickname or a shortened version of "Margaret." Historical records showed that, during that time period, it wasn't uncommon for someone to have the name Margaret and take the name Mary. Her name, Margaret Mary Chaddock, was uncovered, and with that discovery more information began to fall quickly into place.

The team began to use a set of dowsing rods by the large stone pillar, asking the spirit to lead them to the gravesite. After a half hour of following directions through the rods, they found Mary's site next to her husband. To this day, Mary continues to watch over the cemetery, standing fast by the large pillar. She likes to communicate with those who visit the cemetery and often can be sensed using EVP and noticing physical sensations. Sometimes, she can be seen at night roaming through the trees and tombstones, watching both the living and the dead.

Mary isn't the only inhabitant of this cemetery, though. Many nights, visitors can see "walkers" wandering the cemetery grounds. Dark, shadowy figures walking from one place to another and then vanishing. Some are spirits not knowing they have passed, while others are residual energy of events from long ago.

When the cemetery was young, "Mary" tells of the story of a young couple who frequently visited the cemetery, which at that time was located behind a small church. During an investigation one evening, a young psychic named Shayla shared that in her mind's eye she could see the vision of a young woman in her early-to-mid twenties. She had a fair complexion and she wore lots of make-up for that time; her eyes were a dark brown and she had blondish-colored hair. Mary shared with her that the young woman's name was Michelle. Shayla describes the scene as it unfolds: She sees that Michelle was going to the area in the cemetery where the large pillar now resides, the place where Mary always stands watch. Of course, the landscape scene she is seeing in her mind is different then how the land is laid out today. At that time, there was a fence line that was about twenty feet closer than it is now, and across the road from the cemetery once stood a small house or church.

She can see the young woman running across the meadow, through a gravesite that now marks the Ewell family, to the area by the pillar. She spread out a large blanket with a lunch, waiting for someone else to join her. It's not long before a young gentleman wearing a white shirt and dungarees appears from the area that is now wooded. They have their lunch and eventually have relations. The couple don't notice a man watching from across the cemetery, crouched behind a tombstone. As he stands, he appears to be about six foot tall with a large, burly build. He carries what looks like a shotgun. He hastily begins to run across the cemetery, waving the gun at them, yelling, "Get out or I'm going to get you!"

Shayla felt the young woman was a prostitute. She could see Michelle yelling to the young man to run, when a shot was heard. And then another. It wasn't long after that Mary had found the couple and Shayla could see her screaming for help. But none came. Residual energy of this fateful event repeats itself over and over again at various times throughout the day.

When Mary was alive, she had witnessed the double murder of a prostitute and a man. She did not know either of them. The investigators encouraged Mary to take them to the gravesite bearing the murdered couple. She lead the group to the grave site of David C. who died at age sixty years old in April of 1874. She told them that he was never caught and was a "lover" of the prostitute. The two people were killed in a fit of rage, being shot to death. Broken-heartedness was the motive. The year of death was 1854. Research by the team showed that a few years prior to that, local records show a prostitute named Michelle was excommunicated from the church in 1850. David C. was never caught.

According to Mary, David C. also the took blame for some of the Jack The Ripper rumors that occurred in the Batavia area, for his crimes. He killed ten people, but was never caught. Mary described him as a very unassuming person that no one suspected but people did feel was a little sick. She explained that the graves of the prostitute and the murdered man lie beneath a tree to the right of the pillar by which she stands her watch.

An old tale of folklore, maybe. But historical records do verify that the event occurred. Today, if investigators are there at just the right time, they can witness the shadow figures reenacting the event, capture EVPs of gunshots, and sometimes catch a glimpse of a passing mist.

An investigator draws near Mary's pillar and, just prior to being shoved, had this photograph taken. Notice the mist appearing from behind the trees.
Photograph by Dwayne Claud, Western New York Paranormal.

The area around the West Middlebury Cemetery is an area of tremendous spiritual energy. Some theories persist that it's a combination of the faith that lies on this land along with the cemetery; that activity is exacerbated with the power of the Native American influence, since this was a busy trail area for the Seneca Indians. All of this, combined with the flow of an underwater saltwater source, as well as kinetic activity generated by a nearby railway, may be what gives the spirits of West Middlebury Cemetery their ability to manifest. The activity in the cemetery increases dramatically each time a train passes by, especially in latter parts of the evening—although activity has been captured during all times of the day. It's also believed that the cemetery is part of a ley line that runs through the small town of Linden and through another place of great mystery, the Rolling Hills Country Mall.

4

OLD HAUNTS
OF ROCHESTERVILLE

G hosts are not a new phenomenon. Reports of apparitions and spiritual visits are riddled throughout the ages. Rochester, New York, is no different. Newspaper reports spanning over 200 years tell of apparitions that walk the night, noisy ghosts that rattle chains in the darkness. Some buildings still remain although changed by the years, while others are but ghosts themselves of a past long forgotten.

Farmer's Tavern and Inn
(1823-1893)
Main Street and Euclid Street
Rochester, New York

Built as a result of the Erie Canal going through the region, this two-story building served as a place of respite for weary travelers in the area. Although not much by today's standards, each room was a simple 5' x 5' space with holes drilled through the door for ventilation. The inn was filled on a consistent basis, with the exception of one room which was kept vacant because its guests would never stay the night. It was only when the inn was filled to capacity that this room would be rented out to the enjoyment of the locals, who would sit at the bar in the tavern placing bets. Because whoever had the misfortune of getting that room never stayed much past midnight—the spirit would drive them out. There was never a murder in the tavern, although there were many suicides, so it was never determined who the spirit was that haunted the Farmer's Tavern and Inn.

The inn burned down in 1893 along with several other businesses that took up residence on that spot in the years to come. Local anthropologists believed the site may have been one of the many burial mounds that the Senecas had in the region. Nevertheless, the corner of Main Street and now Euclid Avenue became known as a cursed corner or even better known as "Hoodoo Corner." The exact origin of the name is not known but has been referenced in several newspaper articles over the years, including in the obituary of John C. McCurdy of McCurdy's Department Stores. (Keene, 2007)

Hoodoo is a term that was founded in the early nineteenth century in America for African-American folk magic. Folk magic is a world-wide phenomenon. The beliefs and customs brought to America by African slaves mingled here with the beliefs, customs, and botanical knowledge of Native Americans and with the Christian, Jewish, and Pagan folklore of European immigrants. The result was hoodoo. (Yronwade, 2008) As with any religious practices, rituals can be used for good or evil. One common root of Hoodooism is the practice of crossing or jinxing. There have been suggestions that the land on which Midtown Plaza currently resides is cursed land. In 1901, McCurdy looked into purchasing the land where the Farmer's Tavern and Inn was located and building over it to construct his first department store. But he was warned that the corner was cursed and any business placed there suffered great misfortune. This is now the site of the abandoned McCurdy's Department store which was one of the cornerstones of Midtown Plaza. (Keene, 2007) Even to this day, past security guards tell of shadowy figures that walk the building late at night, yet when approached, disappear, and of odd noises and voices that have no explanation.

On July 25, 2008, Midtown Plaza ceased operation. Is this a sign of Hoodoo at work? If you take into consideration that directly across the street from where Midtown Plaza once sat, once resided the First Baptist Church of Rochester—the first church in the city to accept African Americans. It also served as a safe house for the Underground Railroad. If you go back further, several local area anthropologists believe that the site of the old Farmer's Tavern and Inn, then Midtown, sits directly on top of an ancient Seneca burial mound. Folklore or fact, all legends have their basis someplace. One has to wonder about the spiritual power focused in downtown Rochester.

The Powers Building
(Built 1865)
16 West Main Street
Rochester, New York
www.powersbuilding.com

The Powers Building is one of the most remarkable structures in downtown Rochester. It was an engineering marvel. When it was built, it was the tallest building in Rochester featuring acres of

marble, twelve-foot mahogany doors, a fifty-ton spiral cast-iron staircase, the first passenger elevator in Upstate New York, and the first building in Rochester to have electricity utilizing its own boilers for power. Daniel Powers began construction of this building in 1865 as a labor of ego. It was said that he would not allow any buildings in Rochester to be taller. It began as a five-story building, then spanned to thirteen floors with a tower. It was a tourism destination where people could ride to the top of the building to see the sights of Rochester for only a dime a ride up the elevator.

Today, people can take that ride for free and experience the scenic view. But be warned, local rumors have circulated since the turn of the century of the spiritual activity within the building. Sights of a young woman have been seen wandering the corridors. This may be the spirit of Annie Kelly, who according to a newspaper story in 1884, died in a tragic elevator accident in the building. Annie was a laundress in the Powers Building, then known as the Power's Hotel, and while attempting to jump onto a moving elevator, the elevator cut her in half.

Others have reported the figure of a male roaming the building. In fact, Judy Pixley and Dorrie Bjornholm, who run the Buongiorno Café in the center of the atrium, believe it is the ghost of Daniel Powers who roams the building. They tell patrons stories of elevators opening and closing for no reason, ovens turning on and off by themselves and secret passageways behind walls and under the floors within the building itself. In fact, during the renovations of the building back in 1988, several of the security guards who worked in the building refused to patrol above the sixth floor for fear of supernatural activity. (Bryant, 2007)

Think this is just a story? When you step into the Buongiorno Café, there are two old photographs that hang upon the wall showing two figures that can't be explained.

Main Street Armory
(1905)
900 East Main Street
Rochester, New York
www.rochestermainstreetarmory.com

Located directly across the street from the Auditorium Theatre, the Main Street Armory was built in 1905 by the United States Army. This magnificent 138,000 square-foot facility with its landmark seven-story tower was used as a passing point for soldiers in World Wars I and II, preparing them to leave for active duty. In 1943, it was used to house military police for the Army who would oversee local POW Encampments such as those at Cobbs Hill in Rochester, Hamlin, and in Letchworth State Park. At that time, the basement was also used as holding areas for prisoners. In 1990, the National Guard ceased use of the building. For over twenty years, the building's only occupants were some transients who roamed through and pigeons who riddled among the fallen roof timbers. In 2007, local entrepreneur Scott Donaldson purchased the building for $1,000 who later said that if he could have seen the condition the building was in at the time, he wouldn't have purchased it. Donaldson is legally blind, but that will not end his determination of resurrecting the use of the building. He has already invested thousands of dollars into refurbishment of the facility, and it has already begun to host events including Professional Wrestling, the Rochester Raiders Indoor Arena Football, among others. Future plans for the building include the addition of indoor paint ball, a restaurant, coffee house, and an art museum.

Donaldson didn't realize that the purchase of the Armory would come with more than pigeons for tenants. No one told him of the haunted nature of the building. Donaldson said that "because he doesn't have full use of his sight that his other senses are very attuned. He can definitely feel the presence of someone around him when he has been in the building. He tells of workers who have seen shadowy figures walking the main arena floor only to disappear when approached. Doors open and close by themselves and lights turn on and off with no help from a physical person. Some have even reported experiences of being pushed or shoved while in the building.

In November of 2007, Donaldson invited Monroe County Paranormal Investigators, Western New York Paranormal, and Twin Tiers Paranormal to conduct a thorough investigation of the building. Their goal was to collect any scientific evidence of unexplained phenomenon, and through the use of mediums, determine who the spirits might be that are still residing in the Armory. The three teams spread out in the expansive

A view from East Main Street of the Rochester Armory.

Photograph by Dwayne Claud, Western New York Paranormal.

building, conducting their investigation in groups of three to four people each.

Twin Tiers Paranormal, lead by Drew Beeman reported an incident while sitting in the arena area of the now defunct drill hall. According to Beeman, he could feel someone pushing down on his shoulders as he sat in one of the seats, and while this was happening, an object was flung at his feet. He couldn't locate the object after it was thrown, so he wasn't certain what it was, but about the same time this occurred, he visibly watched a light float across the drill hall floor. This was also witnessed by Rob Pistilli of Monroe County Paranormal Investigations. The ball of light appeared to be glowing and spherical in nature. There appeared to be no natural explanation for the light they both viewed. The spherical shape and the self-emitting light of the ball leads them to believe that it was a spirit orb.

It's believed by paranormal researchers that orbs are the simplest form of spirit energy. A basic law of physics is that no energy can be created or destroyed. It can only be transformed from one state into another. The human body contains a constant electrical charge of around 60 Hz. In a variety of life after death experiments, bodies have shown a discharge of energy upon the moment of death along with a small change in body mass. This is allegedly the body releasing the soul's energy. The simplest and most cohesive form of energy that can be formed is a sphere or orb. As the orbs grow larger or more spheres come together, the spirit can manifest into mist, ectoplasm, or even full-form apparitions.

Orbs, however, are very controversial in the field of paranormal research. Skeptical sources explain away the appearance of orbs in photography and video as merely tricks of the camera lens. They believe that they are merely tiny dust particles being lit by the camera flash that are extremely close to the lens. This is true of many of the orb photographs taken by groups; however, closer examination of true spiritual orbs demonstrate that the true orbs show a self-emitting light nature. They contain a nucleus and appear solid. They also move erratically and may show motion in photography.

Investigator Rich Eider of Western New York Paranormal captured this photograph in the basement area of the Armory. The photograph was taken as Eider noticed a shadow movement in the basement. Notice the movement of the orb in the photograph. The flash speed on this camera is approximately 1/500th of a second. The blurred movement of the orb on the photograph shows the tremendous speed of this unexplained object, faster that any dust particle could move.

The basement area proved to be even more interesting for members of the Western New York Paranormal team as they continued their investigation. Members of their team continued to see moving shadow figures in the basement, and at one point, had a light turned on spontaneously in a room they had just left. A room no one else had entered. Investigator Jen Edmiston was recording video and audio that evening, and while in the basement she recorded two very disturbing pieces of electronic voice phenomenon. If you recall from my earlier explanation, electronic voice phenomenon are "ghost voices." Paranormal researchers use digital or audio recording devices while they are in haunted locations to ask questions. After the investigations, they review the audio and it is not uncommon for voices to respond to their questions responses that investigators don't hear while they are there on site.

On this evening, Edmiston asked in the basement if there were any guns left down there. After review of the tape, the response was, "We have three left." She then asked why the spirits remained in the building, and it replied, "We wait for Rob." Rob was the lead investigator for Monroe County Paranormal Investigators. He had yet to make it to the basement, nor would he on that night. Sometimes investigators know where they should go and where they shouldn't. Tonight was a night Rob decided it would be best to not venture into the basement despite being beckoned there.

Alexander Pope once wrote, "Fools rush in where angels fear to tread." It's an important philosophy to remember when investigating any location. trust your instincts and feelings. If there's a sense that you are not wanted in a location, then chances are it is a place that you shouldn't be. For there are more in the realm of the spiritual world than just energies of departed souls.

Eastman Dental Dispensary
(1917)
800 East Main Street
Rochester, New York

Built in 1917, the Eastman Dental Dispensary was funded by George Eastman of the Eastman Kodak Company. It contributed greatly to the improvement of dentistry in the United States and Europe by providing a training ground for dentists and hygienists. It became one of the leading schools for dentistry in the country very quickly while providing the underprivileged free dental care. It was the first free dentistry clinic in the United States with thirty-seven operating units. The Dispensary closed in 1976 when the school was formally moved to the University of Rochester.

The building was purchased in 2007 by Scott Donaldson, with the plan of demolishing the building to make room for new business, but since the building is on the "Most Endangered List" of historical buildings, he has been unable to proceed. Instead, he has invested money in the partial renovation of the building which includes five floors along with a basement and sub-basement. In an interview with 13WHAM News, workers have reported that the building appears haunted. Apparently the workers doing renovations in the building have heard strange noises coming from the upper floors.

One worker, Vic DePaula, said, "I've been here alone before at night working, and it's just very distracting—just the building and the atmosphere it has." A skeptic might suggest animal activity, but foreman David Gray said, that when they "walk around, haven't seen anything; no droppings, no tracks in the dust—there is nothing indicating there's an animal in here. But, there is something up there that is kind of creepy. I don't like being in here alone when that thing's up there growling." This is a growling which comes from an area near the west staircase between the third and fourth floors.

Donaldson called in the Western New York Paranormal team along with Mystic Encounters Investigations to conduct a night of research in the building. With it being such a large building, the teams split up, with Western New York Paranormal heading to the basement and Mystic Encounters heading towards the top floors. The building is very deteriorated. Years of disuse have taken their toll on this piece of Rochester's history. The team ran across no type of paranormal activity in the basement, although it was riddled with empty cages. In its day, the Dispensary conducted animal research and these cages are all that are left of that past—or so the team thought. Maybe what hunts the corridors of this old landmark are not the souls of humans, but the energies of animals that have since died.

It wasn't until the team went to the third floor that the building started to come alive. One of the members of Western New York Paranormal, Tammy Conley, sensed the presence of a young child playing around one of the stairwells. She was described as brown haired and wearing a dress. Later in the evening, the psychic from the Mystic Encounters team verified this feeling, sensing the same spirit. The spirit was described as a residual spirit by both mediums, the energy signature of a spirit who is unaware of anyone that surrounds them.

The stairwell was approached between the third and fourth floors, and there was an immediate sensation of unease for members of both teams. The psychic from the Mystic Encounters team heard the sound of a growl. It was described as animal-like in nature, but there were no animals there that could possibly be making the noise. Not long after that encounter, the Western New York Paranormal team was in that area and felt the sensation of being unwanted. Investigator Liza Eider took a photograph into a room just adjacent to the stairwell which appeared to be some type of lab room at one time. After further investigation, the image of an animal was seen peering through the window back at her. It resembled that of a primate. (This image is available by visiting the gallery section for Haunted Rochester at www.wnyparanormal.org.) Could that possibly be the spirit that was guarding the stairwell? Could it have been a spirit of one of the many animals used for experimentation at the dispensary?

The investigators determined that night that there is a lot of spiritual energy running through the building. It contains residual energy patterns of the past replaying over and over again like an old movie, but it also contains some elements that aren't happy with the intrusion of man. Perhaps it's one of the animal spirits or something even darker.

Burlington Coat Factory
286 Greece Ridge Center Drive
Greece, New York

Looking for a ghostly experience while shopping in Greece? You may want to try the Burlington Coat Factory. Staff at the store tell of ghostly customers who are there one moment and then disappear when approached. Darting shadows and figures are not uncommon in this store, so when someone walks up to you, be careful: they may not be an employee or customer. They may just be a past resident of the area.

Fairport Village Hall
31 South Main Street
Fairport, New York

This building, constructed in 1906, had multiple uses. The basement floor served as the jail for the area while the first and second floors held municipal offices. The third floor housed a movie theater up until 1920. Today, it is home to the police department, justice court, and other government offices. There have been multiple reports over the past years though of a long-past judge that still haunted the court room in this building with unexplained shadows moving throughout the hallways. Perhaps there is still justice on the other side.

The DeLand Chemical Company
Lift Bridge Lane
Fairport, New York

A building originally built by the DeLand Chemical Company in the mid-1800s, canal side in the village of Fairport, still remains as a professional office space and location for many retail companies. The company, at that time, produced baking soda and employed hundreds of people in the factory. It was an industry that boomed in this small Erie canal village. Local lore suggests, though, that in 1872, the owner D.B. DeLand fell to his death in one of the operating elevators in the building.

In 1893, a disastrous fire struck the DeLand Chemical Company that leveled several buildings in the plant and took several lives. The exact cause of the fire was never determined. It was six years later that a second fire struck the same plant, then used by the Chase Flour Company, that began in the bowels of the building's boiler room. Mysterious fires have riddled the history of the Box Factory since its construction nearly 150 years ago.

Today, mysterious happenings surround the tenants of the building. Elevators travel between floors only to have their doors open with no passengers. Some believe this to be the spirit of D.B. DeLand himself who still walks the factory. In fact, a past tenant reported that as they were leaving the building one night, a cold chill passed across them and they heard a deep voice call to them. As they looked around, no one was seen—until they looked up to a window that overlooked the lobby area. In that window a dark shadow figure was seen watching from above. Within seconds of being noticed by the tenant, the figure vanished into thin air.

Some individuals have reported the smell of smoke in the hallways on the upper floors of the office building. It has been described as the smell of smoke from a fire. When they noticed the smell, a heaviness in the chest and difficulty breathing come over them. These are feelings that happen on occasion, and as quickly as they come, they pass.

In 2005, Western New York Paranormal was asked to investigate selected areas of the building for unexplained activities. A tenant at the time reported unexplained voices in their office suite that sounded much like that of a child. Objects would move on their own and shadow figures would be noticed moving throughout the suite when no one else was there.

The team set up a variety of cameras and recorders throughout the suite in hopes of catching some evidence of paranormal activity. Two investigators were left in the suite to conduct EVP recordings and take photographs while video cameras also ran surveillance and the remaining members of the team began working through the other areas of the building.

Most paranormal investigations are uneventful. It isn't until the investigators actually go back and review their recordings and photographs that they find evidence of activity. This is one of those very unusual cases where something actually did happen while the investigators sat, questioned, and watched. They sat in an office space where there had been reported activity of object movement and they began their EVP recording session. They asked simple questions such as "What is your name?" and "What year is it?" when a chair in the office very slowly began to rock back and forth on its own, back and forth, with no noted external force moving it. This was also one of the very unusual times when an investigator actually had a video recorder focused on the area so the movement was captured on video.

Later that night, a psychic investigator came into the suite and began picking up on a spirit of a child of about five or six years of age whose name was "Reggie." This investigator felt the child was there simply because he liked the attention and the fact that people would play with him there. What makes the name more significant is that when the recordings were reviewed from the first set of investigators, the name "Reggie" was spoken in a very low, child-like voice responding to the question about the entity's name.

While in the basement, multiple investigative teams encountered an entity who became known as "Arthur" by the psychic investigators. While in the boiler room area of the basement, investigators noticed the movement of a shadowy figure at the far end of the room. As they would approach, the entity would back away and recede into the shadows. Until they came to a storage room, and when they entered the room, investigators could feel an overwhelming presence there with a chill in the air. When they left the room, the feelings didn't leave with them. It was if that room was "Arthur's place." One of the investigators asked for "Arthur" to give them a sign of his presence—for him to knock on something so that they would know that he was there. Moments passed. Moments that seemed like hours. Then it happened, "ting...ting...bang." It was the sound of something knocking on the paint cans stacked in the storage room. Quickly the investigators entered the room to see what could have been making the noise. But there was nothing. Just the paint cans stacked in the corner. They back away from the room again and asked for "Arthur" to show them another sign. It happened again, "ting...bang...ting." They asked for him to bang twice, "bang...bang." The psychic investigator there began to communicate with the spirit and they gathered that Arthur had died in the building. He died from a fire that had begun down in this very room from some oil-soaked rags that had been thrown near the boiler. The boiler ignited them and the fire started that burned down DeLand Chemical. Separate teams throughout the night explored this same area, independent of the knowledge of the other investigators...hearing the same noises, "ting... ting...bang."

The team felt that, in walking the building, there were many other residual spirits that wandered through it. None that were there to cause harm, just energies from those long passed. One does have to wonder though, why the string of fires throughout the building's history? Is there something on that land that doesn't want the building there or is it just a string of coincidences? Another coincidence, or perhaps fate, happened as the team from Western New York Paranormal was leaving the building. They noticed a photograph in the hall showing the factory and several of the buildings along the canal. It showed the burnt ashes of the building. The photo was dated February 4, 1887. The date of this particular investigation was February 4, 2006. It was exactly one 129 years to the day after the fire had occurred.

Charlotte-Genesee Lighthouse
70 Lighthouse Street
Rochester, New York
www.geneseelighthouse.org

In 1822, the original lighthouse and keeper's house was constructed on just over three acres of land on what is now Lighthouse Road. The lighthouse itself was whitewashed with a small two-room keeper's house made of stone. This lighthouse remained in operation until 1884, when a cast iron lighthouse was built to replace it, but was dismantled after only three years and moved to Ohio. In its place was built a twenty-eight-foot wooden-frame lighthouse. One evening when keeper George Codding spent the night in the tower, it was very cold. It required him to burn the floor boards of the keeper's house. Later, the building was torn down and just the tower remains today. Stories now circulate of a phantom light house keeper that roams the building.

Lift Bridge
Main Street
Fairport, New York

The lift bridge in Fairport has mysterious lore that surrounds it. It has become known as the "singing bridge" since its construction, due to the array of moans and groans that it makes as the gates lift and close. Many people feel they hear sounds like voices from beyond the grave. It was back in the 1950s that a local preacher climbed the railings of the bridge and began to sing hymns and preach the gospel until he mysteriously fell to his death, despite the efforts of local law enforcement to save his life. One has to wonder, was this preacher attempting to quiet or release the spirits from the bridge? There are still reports, on occasion, of people seeing a floating blue light around the bridge on dark fall nights.

Rolling Hills Country Mall
1101 Bethany Center Road
East Bethany, New York
www.rollinghills-ghosthunt.com

The Rolling Hills Country Mall, located approximately an hour south of Rochester, is an enigma in the world of the paranormal. It can be easily be compared to other public haunts such as the Moundsville Penitentiary in West Virginia, the Mansfield State Reformatory in Ohio, and even the Stanley Hotel in Colorado. Historical records show that the property was an old stage coach stop before the property was purchased in 1826 by Genesee County, who then opened it as a poorhouse. Throughout the nineteenth century, the location served as an asylum for the insane as well as an orphanage. By the 1940s, the property had become a nursing home. It was finally closed down in 1974. (Borick, 2006)

There is a lot of mystery and legend that surrounds this property and building. In fact, while the building was operating as an asylum and orphanage, rumors ran rampant that a coven of witches operated within the walls of the institution. Now not all witches are bad, many are just misunderstood. These

individuals, however, worshiped the dark arts and there were suggestions made by many of the locals of that time that rituals were held within the building itself, rituals that included magic and infant sacrifice. Many of these events occurred on the fourth floor of the building where the nurses had their living

Once a poor house, now home for many restless spirits.

quarters. The allegations of witchcraft and sacrifice can not be substantiated; however, when the building was undergoing some repair of the fourth floor, a local worker discovered a ring hidden within the walls—a ring that was silver and had the face of a horned creature on it, a common symbol of demonic worship. It was discovered in the room where the head nurse resided.

Through the decades, rumors of haunting continued to circulate regarding this building and its property. Teenagers would break into the building to try to scare each other, some even performing rituals on the top floor. Passersby would see an older woman sitting in an old wicker wheelchair in one of the overlooks. She would just smile and wave as cars would pass by. Individuals entering the building would hear strange noises, doors closing, chairs moving around by themselves—all without explanation.

It was in 2004 that one of the first paranormal investigation teams entered the building. The Paranormal and Ghost Society, a Buffalo-based organization, brought their team of investigators armed with cameras to see what mysteries that they could unlock within the walls of the building. Interestingly, they were the first group to capture photographs of mist and ectoplasm at the building. As time went on, other groups began to come and investigate as well.

In 2005, Western New York Paranormal began their initial investigations of the property. One evening, the organization had planned a brief meeting on-site to discuss group business. During the meeting, one of the investigators, Bill, kept looking over into the darkness. Quietly he said, "They're not happy we're here." Yet the meeting continued. At the end, Bill was heading towards the stairwell. He was determined to get to the fourth floor. As he reached the stairwell, he turned to other investigators and said, "They're killing them. I have to do something!" and began to climb the stairs. His eyes had a look unlike anything that any of the investigators had ever seen before. It was a blank look with nothing behind the eyes.

One of the investigators grabbed Bill's hand, stopping him from climbing the stairs and explaining that it was important for Bill to the leave the building. He needed to leave and ground himself. But Bill was intent. Several other members of the organization heard the commotion and came to help. They led Bill back down the stairs and towards the main doors. As he was going down the stairs, one of the investigators stopped in his tracks—turning to look behind him up the stairs—and then began praying in Hebrew, as the others took Bill outside of the building.

In the parking lot, Bill seemed to calm back down and relax. After taking a few deep breaths, he seemed fine. Since the excitement appeared to be over, one investigator who had a tape recorder on him went into the building to grab some additional equipment that had been left there. As he did, he approached another researcher and made the comment that he thought Bill had just been possessed. Suddenly, the main door burst open again. Bill was hastily coming through the doorway heading straight back towards the stairwell with a number of individuals following him. Three men grabbed him, forcing him down into a chair.

"You need to relax, Bill," one of the investigators said. Bill responded, "There is no Bill here. Only Thomas. And you will let me go before I put you in the grave." Held down, the group began prayer, over and over again they said the *Lord's Prayer*. One individual began commanding the entity to leave in the name of Christ, only to be responded to by vulgarities. Soon, he was approached by a pair of Pagans who had come to the meeting that evening. One of them, with crystals in hand, came to Bill while channeling her spirit guide. She commanded that Thomas leave him. The spirit had no right to the body. It had no choice but to leave. After some time, the spirit left and Bill was taken home.

It sounds like the storyline of a horror movie, but it happened. It was captured on audio and video. When investigators went back and reviewed the audio, they found a bone-chilling EVP. At the time the investigator had made the comment that he thought Bill had been possessed, there was a response on the tape recorder. It was a low, gravely, inhuman, serpentine-sounding voice saying, "Yessssssssss." As the Pagans demanded the entity leave, video recording was going on, and as the entity left, a visible spirit orb was witnessed rising up out of Bill.

Although there are fear-filled stories that have occurred at Rolling Hills, there have also been some very touching stories as well. In one of the first public ghost hunts at the location, a woman had come with the hopes of contacting a family member who had long since passed there. She explained that her Grandmother had once been a patient at the nursing home and had died in the facility. She had suffered a fall in one of the stairways.

It was early in the night when she made it down to where the cafeteria once was, and she was feeling a bit disappointed

A ghostly presence waiting to be acknowledged.
Photograph by Sandy Heglund, Western New York Paranormal.

A spirit wandering the grounds. *Photograph by Nora Ballard.*

that she hadn't seen any signs of her grandmother. She had experienced odd feelings in different places, but found nothing she could really validate. One of the investigator/guides was in the cafeteria at that time and walked over to her with a compass in hand. He explained to her how sometimes spirits can be found using compasses. The fact that spirits are energy allows them to manipulate magnetic fields and sometimes an individual standing completely still could experience the compass of a needle moving back and forth as much as five or ten degrees. Usually, that would mean that there was paranormal activity in the area. Being a bit of a skeptic, she took the compass in hand and asked the question out loud, "Are you here, grandma?" She looked down, and as she did, the compass began to move. It didn't move just five or ten degrees. It spun completely around several times, three hundred and sixty degrees. And the woman began to cry. "Grandma," she said. She then used that compass to find the place in the building where her grandmother had died, and placed a single rose at the spot. "Grandma, go to God now," she said. Her trip to the building had been complete.

5

THAT'S "SPIRIT"-TAINMENT

The theatre has long since been a world shrouded in superstition and ghost lore. Some speculate that because the actors put so much energy into creating the characters they portray on stage, that the characters take on a life of their own, living even after the theatre remains empty. As is a standing tradition in the theatre, they choose one day a week to close the production—a superstition that allows one day for the ghosts in the theatre to perform the roles that the actors created for them, also conveniently giving the actors one day off after a long series of performances.

One other interesting note is that the spirit Thespis holds honor among the actors. Thespis was the first person ever to speak individual lines on stage as an actor, hence referring now to thespians as actors. It was estimated that his first performance was on November 23, 534 BC. Should any playful unexplained phenomenon occur during a production, then Thespis usually takes the blame.

Fun lore or ghostly truth? Each theatre has their own tales to tell. The theatre district of Rochester, New York, is one full of plays to act and stories to share. Grab your ticket and enjoy the show!

Geva Theatre Centre
75 Woodbury Boulevard
Rochester, New York
www.gevatheatre.org

Built in 1865 by Andrew J. Warner as a Naval Armory, the building served as a defense site to protect Rochester and the Erie Canal from any potential invasion from Great Britain. The Armory saw little military action, so in 1906, the building became the first convention center in Rochester. It was later turned into an emergency hospital in 1918, during an influenza pandemic which took the lives of many Rochesterians. It was estimated that in just one week alone over 238 individuals died as a result of this outbreak in Rochester—many of which may have been housed at this armory. In six weeks, a total of 30,736 deaths were reported. The actual number of influenza-related deaths during this period was probably much higher. For 1918, the overall death rate in New York State was among the highest ever recorded for the state. Mayors banned public funerals and required all bodies to be buried within twenty-four hours of their deaths to avoid further spread of the disease. One would have to wonder if such a quick burial with no chance for loved ones to say their farewells, would sit well with the recently departed. Many of them may still be waiting to say their farewells to family members.

After the pandemic, the building went unused for several decades, but in 1982, renovations began to create the Geva Theatre Center as it is today. Hundreds attend live performances every week, but many don't realize that the performances they are attending could be watched by a cast of unseen characters. Performers tell tales of unexplained noises, shadowy figures that appear on the stage, and even of ghostly audience members that appear during rehearsals.

In the fall of 2007, a joint paranormal investigation was coordinated at the Geva Theatre Center utilizing researchers from Monroe County Paranormal Investigators and Western

New York Paranormal of Rochester. The intentions of the investigation was to document any unexplained phenomena in the building and attempt to either verify the findings or mark them as unexplained.

Jennifer Edmiston, a member of Western New York Paranormal, reported several experiences while in the main theatre at Geva. While in the balcony section, she felt as if someone was physically behind her pushing her forward in the seat. She described the feeling like someone had placed their hands on her shoulders and were pushing her forward. It wasn't with great force, but great pressure. It was at this time another investigator took a photograph which revealed a fine mist around Edmiston. Shortly after that incident, she spotted two figures in the main stage area. A dark figure walked in front of the stage. She described it as "coloring book-like, but not colored in." It was brief, lasting only a second or two, but she was positive of what she had seen and experienced.

Investigators reported unexplained noises throughout the entire evening. The noises would seem to move when investigators attempted to locate them, making them unable to identify any physical cause. These were captured on audio recordings though and later identified as the sounds of chains. When these sounds were analyzed, they were found to resonate above the sound of human hearing. Why would the sounds of chains be heard? It sounds like a very stereotypical sound for a building that would be haunted and there has yet to be a photograph taken of a spirit wearing chains. The exception of course is Jacob Marley from the play *A Christmas Carol,* but perhaps that is where the inspiration comes for the spirit to produce the sounds. Could it come from a play that is performed time and time again, year after year? Or could the sounds being produce be that of sounds that are normally heard backstage such as curtains rising and falling? It could also be remnant energy from a hospital long ago that was once in that location. Who can really say for certain?

The most fascinating finding of the night was discovered in the basement with a photograph captured by investigators Chuck and Robin Wilson of Monroe County Paranormal Investigators, in an area where team psychics felt very uncomfortable. Upon closer examination of the photograph, a dark figure can be seen peering through the doorway. The figure has the appearance of a grim reaper and was unseen at the time by investigators. (You however can see this entity by visiting the gallery section of Haunted Rochester at www.wnyparanormal.org.) So it seems there truly is a phantom of this theatre house.

Auditorium Theatre
875 East Main Street
Rochester, New York
www.rbtl.org

Many don't realize this majestic building, constructed in 1866, was home to the first Masonic Temple in Rochester, New York. The building had large meeting rooms and several theatres, with membership stretching out to the Buffalo region. The building was an active lodge until 2002 when the brethren opted not to renew their lease and moved to a different building.

Through the 136-year history, there have been several tragedies within the building, including two major fires which caused substantial damage. There were no reported injuries, but such tragic events can lead a building to breathe a life of its own. There are also questions that arise around the secrecy of any Masonic organization, including suspected reports of magical rites during ceremonies. Of course, the books of the Masons are closed to non-members so this can not be substantiated in any manner whatsoever.

As is part of the Mason tradition, many live performances were presented at the building on their many stages. The building has four main stages within its walls, though only two

A view from East Main Street of the Auditorium Theatre.

are currently used. Not much has changed in these theatres since they were built. Certainly, small improvements or modifications here and there, but the only substantial difference is the absence of the "ghost lights" for the stages. Performers are very superstitious individuals. As mentioned earlier, it's the belief of many that so much energy is given into a performance that the characters live on after the play ends, reliving their greatest moments on stage. The "ghost light" remains lit within the theatre at all times so the stage is never dark. If the light is out, the spirits can't return and will cause accidents and strange occurrences around productions. One of the first things that head steward Gary Zaccarai did some thirty years ago when he began his job at the theatre was to remove the fabled "ghost lights." He felt it was outdated and served no real purpose in the theatre—or did it?

Although Zaccarai doesn't recall any strange accidents related to the productions, he does remember a story his electrician told him. Back in the early 80s, there had been a death in the theatre. It occurred in a small room just off the theatre's boiler room in the basement. As he tells the story, a worker from a local utility company had been brought in to do some work on the electrical system in the theatre. The theatre, being as old as it was, had the old bus type of fuses, which could be very dangerous to anyone touching them. As the electrician entered the room, his tool belt brushed upon one of the open fuses and he was electrocuted. Now, many may have brushed this story off as just another urban legend, but Zaccarai isn't so certain. While in that area of the basement, he has witnessed a dark shadowy figure moving around from the corner of his eye and has heard sounds he can't explain.

Paranormal activity doesn't just remain in the bowels of this historic landmark of Rochester. A gentleman has been seen walking in the lobby area of the theatre. Zaccari describes him as having a medium build and wearing a blue jacket. He recalls one day that he was working inside the theatre and glanced up to see this gentleman walking past the entry door into one of the main theatres. Confused because the doors were locked into the building, Zaccarai went to go speak to the gentleman—only to find that no one was there. Perhaps this may have been a trick of the light, or perhaps a long-since-passed patron of the theatre awaits the next show.

But like any theatre, there are always stories of specters and ghosts in the performance areas; and the Auditorium Theatre is no different. It's not uncommon for the stage to be used for dress rehearsals for local singers and bands. Zaccarai tells of two occasions where the performers actually had spectral spectators watching the performance. One musician that spoke with Zaccarai believes that he watched shadowy figures in the theatre seats watching his musical group practice one evening and then towards the end of the practice, simply stood up and vanished. Zaccarai's own daughter witnessed a dark woman watching her sing one evening from stage left, only to disappear into the shadows.

Western New York Paranormal had the opportunity take in a small group to investigate the theatre. The team was assembled and they arrived shortly before the appointed time. Their guides were happy to have them there, and eagerly showed the team the several places they'd been invited to investigate—the main theater and the basement level.

In The Basement

The first place the team examined was the basement. They were shown several rooms with reported activity, which included several storage areas and the boiler room. It was just outside of one of the large storage areas that the sensitive of the group received her first impressions. "I got my first impression, and based on the limited history that I know of the place, it wasn't the impression I might have expected," said Sarah. She explained that the team was scouting for video, trying for EVPs and taking photographs...while she took a few steps out of the storage room to refocus. At this time, she was now standing just outside the doorway to the boiler room and the storage room.

"As I stood there, I was shown the visual of a wizened old man. He was hunched over and wandering around the hallway. I was given a name that sounded like 'Todd' with this man. His clothes were well worn, but not tattered—just old and kind of grimy, like you'd find clothes after years and years of use. A sunken face and a slightly grumpy attitude accompanied this man," said Sarah. She described him to the team, and they began asking questions of him—hoping for a response. One of the questions asked was, "Does it bother you that we're here?" The response she heard was, "Leave me alone." After a few more questions were asked, like, "Why are you here?" and "What is your name?" she distinctly heard the spirit moan, "Leave me *alonnnne*. This is my place and I do things my way down here."

The energy changed quickly after that. The room felt much lighter and quieter, as if the entity had simply faded away. The team moved over to the boiler room next. It was here that many years ago an RG&E employee electrocuted himself and died. Nothing seemed amiss in this room; it was as spiritually clean as it could be.

In the Theater

Shortly thereafter, the team moved upstairs to the main theater. This is where the rest of the investigation would take place. Sarah and Stacie sat at center stage, watching the many rows of seats in front of and above them. It was utterly still and quiet.

Soon, things began to catch the corner of Sarah's eye towards the right side of the theater. Small flashes of light seemed to be moving. She sat there for awhile longer, letting her eyes roam across the floor seating and mezzanine. "Suddenly, my eyes were pulled to the back right side of the theater. I watched as a shadowy form strode from the aisle to the wall, and seemingly disappeared right through the wall! Well that was interesting, I thought to myself," said Sarah. Sarah then moved to that area of seats and sat there for awhile, noting that the area felt energetically heavy; however, soon after I sat down, the energy changed and felt completely normal again.

After that, Sarah moved back to the stage and sat for a few more minutes with Stacie. Lights and movements continued to catch Sarah's eye from stage right. Stacie began to take photographs in that direction as temperature fluctuations ran rampant. "One moment you're cool and comfortable, the next you're scorching hot—and you haven't even moved from your spot," said Sarah. There is plenty of residual energy in the building from the many performances and activities that have been held there. Several members of the team heard moans and, at one point, Sarah was sure she heard applause. However, no specific entities approached Sarah while we were in the main theater. She wondered if this was because

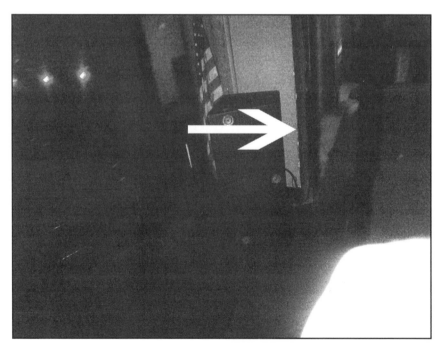

The spirit of "Bobby" taking one last curtain call.
Photograph by Stacie Barry, Western New York Paranormal.

the residual energy levels were so strong; the theater itself seemed to hum with an energy all it's own.

As the team was preparing to go, they were able to discuss the findings with their guides, who were more than eager to know if the team had found anything worthwhile. Sarah described the entity that she met in the basement, and was met with jaws dropping. "That's Tom! Little Tommy!" they cried. They went on to describe an old, ninety-four-year-old man that literally used to "haunt" the theater. He would come every day, bringing his coffee and spinning the same old tales that they'd all heard time and time again. He was finally restricted from entering the building, as its owners were afraid he might pass on while inside. As Sarah described the man and what he'd said to her, she was met with smiles. "Oh yes, that sounds just like Tommy; he definitely was possessive of this place." It was an outstanding validation for Sarah. The "Todd" she'd met just a few hours before was actually "Tom," a keeper of the building he so dearly loved in life.

Are these stories just hallucinations caused by lights playing tricks on the eyes? Could it perhaps be the disappearance of the "ghost light" from the theatre itself that has made the spirits restless or is it just the need to have one last ghostly curtain call?

Frontier Field
1 Morrie Silver Way
Rochester, NY
www.redwingsbaseball.com

Baseball fans have a reputation of complete dedication to their favorite team. The fans of the Rochester Red Wings are no different. According to the Red Wing's Media Relations Director, Manager Chuck Hinkle, in 1998, the ball club received what they thought was a very a unique request: to have a deceased man's ashes spread across the field. The request itself was not unusual because across the country fans have asked to have their ashes spread across the baseball field to show their dedication to their team. What made this request unique was the fact that this man was homeless and had no living relatives. A local family he had befriended approached the management of the team because they knew of this man's love for baseball. The field was happy to accommodate the fan. Soon after, another request came from another family, then another, and then another. Today, the ball park reviews each request, and if it is off-season considers approving the request. The spreading of ashes among the bases has just added to the ghostly reputation that the ballpark has gained since its construction.

In October 2005, ESPN sportscaster Don Barone decided to look into the rumors of Frontier Field being haunted with assistance from local paranormal investigator Joe Burkhart and his team from Rochester Paranormal. The investigation began for the team out by the first baseline. The team focused with cameras and recorders, Burkhart called for the spirits of the game to make their presence known, and suddenly, a gust of wind came from nowhere. And the game begins. Psychic investigator Cindy Lee takes pictures as Burkhart continues to rally the spirits of the game. According to the report, she tells Barone that she senses spirits of long-passed players from the twenties and thirties still playing the game that they loved, and that fans who were dedicated to the game still reside in the stadium cheering on the players. It seems that once you're a baseball fan, then you're always a baseball fan—at least if you are a Red Wings fan in Rochester.

6

BEDS, SPOOKS, AND "SPIRITS"

W ho hasn't been on a vacation that they wished would never end? One where you may have found a welcoming bed and breakfast tucked away from the world with a favorite restaurant not far away. A restaurant that may have had a unique atmosphere all its own, or one so familiar that you called it home. A vacation filled with people that made you feel like family.

In Rochester, there are still many who remain at their favorite haunts, waiting to welcome you home.

Applebee's
200 Paddy Creek Circle
Greece, New York

Where the Applebee's sits today on Paddy Creek Drive was the location of a tragic hotel fire in November of 1978. A fire roared through the fifteen-year-old Holiday Inn early in the morning of November 26, 1978, at approximately 2:45 am—close to the witching hour, the true "dead of night." Contrary to the belief of many individuals, the true witching hour, or dead of night, is not midnight. It is around 3 am. This is the time when the veil is thinnest between realms and dark entities are at their strongest power. In many ways,

A place for food, family and "spirits."

it is a mockery of the trinity and an exact opposite time of when Christ died on the cross. Did the time of the fire have anything to do with this? It does make you wonder, but reports from a local fire department report that the blaze began in the basement, spreading quickly through all three floors of the fully-occupied Holiday Inn, with not one alarm sounding to warn the guests. Flames shot over 100 feet in the air as the hotel burned, forcing guests to trample each other in a panic as they escaped, while others were jumping from second-story windows. Over a dozen fire companies were called to the scene to help. In the end, ten died in the blaze with twenty-five injured. Of those who died, there was one young girl and her mother.

The tragedy was long forgotten as time moved on. Progress and new business entered into the Greece area over the years to come, and Applebee's was one such business. Applebee's is known for its great selection of appetizers, but this restaurant has a small attraction of its own that many people don't know about. This Applebee's restaurant is the home to the spirit of a young girl. One evening in March of 2004, a young Allison Higgins was playing with the cellular phone of a friend of the family. She was only eight years old and was amazed by the fact that a telephone could take photographs, so she was clicking cell phone pictures in the entire restaurant of friends, family, and people she didn't even know—until one surprising photograph was captured; it was the photograph of a young girl. A young girl with long blonde hair around the age of eight appeared to be floating about the lights in the restaurant in a kneeling position with her head bowed. This young girl was wearing a pinkish-red nightgown and appeared to be in prayer.

Could this have been the spirit of the young girl who died in the 1978 hotel fire just across the street? Could it be the spirit of the young girl that dances on the stage of the church across the street in the Childtime Learning Center? Or could it be just the energy of a child praying so hard for God to hear that the message is still being sent?

The Reunion Inn
4565 Culver Road
Rochester, New York

Steve Sah, one of the owners of the Reunion Inn, claims he had a very unexpected encounter in the basement of his restaurant over thirty years ago. As he tells the story, he was all alone on a cold December morning when he felt boney fingers grab his elbow. Startled, he swung around only to find himself still alone. Frightened, he ran to the walk-in cooler and stayed inside until he couldn't stand the cold anymore. Getting up enough nerve, Steve ran back upstairs and held the secret for some time until a co-worker shared the exact same story.

Several others have also experienced mysterious happenings in the basement of the Reunion Inn. Employees have experienced trays flying off shelves, voices saying, "good morning," at times when the building was empty. Even the patrons have seen a few things. The most interesting activity seems to take place in a small dining area upstairs. One couple dining there claimed to have seen a woman wearing a gown appear in front of them. And when spoken to, she faded back into the woodwork. This area is adjacent to a small storage room where many psychics and mediums have all agreed that something evil resides. There are rumors of a death that may have occurred in that room long ago from an illness, or could it be the spirits of those whose bodies used to reside in the small private cemetery plot behind the building? According to the local historian, Patricia Wagner, the bodies were moved in 1865, from the area that now is the parking lot for the nearby ice cream shop. They were moved to St. Anne's Cemetery across the street, but who really knows for certain if all the bodies made the move or whether there are still those that remained behind?

The Green Lantern Inn
One East Church Street
Fairport, New York
www.thegreenlanterninn.com

The Green Lantern Inn was built in 1875 by Henry Deland, who was a local wealthy philanthropist. The home was one of the first in the region that was built with indoor plumbing for running water and pipelines for gas lights. This one-of-a-kind home was built for around $50,000 and was the home of the Deland family for approximately seventeen years. It was in 1892 that Deland lost his fortune. He had invested heavily in farmland in Florida, and when farmers defaulted on land lease payments, he was left penniless.

The house went through the hands of several individuals throughout the years until 1927 when the home became the Green Lantern Inn.

Over the years, there have been reports from employees and patrons alike of strange occurrences in the establishment, and passersby have noticed on some nights that there is a lone candle lit, seen from the cupola with the figure of a male beckoning. Some say this is the spirit of Henry Delund. Although the new owners report no such occurrence in the building, in 2006, they brought in the Mystic Encounters Paranormal Team to dispel the urban legend once and for all.

Mystic Encounters brought with them their team of scientific investigators, along with a local psychic, to conduct a thorough paranormal investigation of the building. The team had several experiences that they couldn't explain during the investigation. In the basement, one investigator had their hair tugged by an unseen force. On the second floor, in an area where the servant's quarters were once located, flying orbs of light were caught on video. It was also in this area that an investigator reported a coldness on his arm that lasted for several moments. The psychic felt is was a child holding the investigator's arm. When evidence was reviewed, there was a child's voice that could be heard on the audio recorder with a plea for "help." But perhaps one of the more compelling pieces of evidence was captured in the main banquet room with a photograph taken by one of the Mystic Encounters investigators of a full-form apparition in a mirror in the room. The photo depicts a long white flowing gown. It was at the same time other investigators reported seeing darting lights about the banquet room.

Did the Mystic Encounters team catch a ghostly apparition in a mirror or was it just lens flare? And what about the young child holding the investigator's arm, asking for help? Is the Green Lantern Inn hunted? This team believes that the original owner, Henry Deland, still roams the halls along with the residual energies of around twenty other spirits...giving this restaurant a new twist on offering food and "spirits."

Springbrook Inn
26 North Street
Caledonia, New York
www.thespringbrookinn.com

When the lights go out, sometimes the activity continues throughout the night at the Springbrook Inn in Caledonia. One former bartender tells of a night that she working alone in the restaurant. She was tending bar and talking with a regular customer when both began to hear horrible noises coming from the kitchen. When they opened the door to the kitchen, they were witness to three large fish tubs being hurled across the floor. She was the only employee there. That in itself was unusual because normally the dining room was filled with customers, many of which have been waited on over the past thirty years by waitress Sue Grant.

Grant also tells of one night when the cook was preparing food and the steam table kept being turned off while she heard the kitchen door opening and closing with noises of someone working behind it. Aditionally, place settings at tables have been completely changed when no one else has been in the building. Customers have even been exposed to some of the activity with place cards flying off the table on one occasion.

Once a stagecoach stop in the 1800s, the Springbrook Inn now is a restaurant and local landmark. A destination that some psychics believe still houses guests from another time. In an interview with *R-News*, one local psychic found that her hand began to write a message on its own, a process known as automatic writing. Automatic writing allows a spirit to communicate with the living by using the hand of a medium to write a message with pen and paper. While sitting in the bar area of the establishment, she received the message, "Tell my mother that Nettie died." Just one of the many spirits trying to communicate to the living at the Springbrook Inn. The psychic who encountered this communication believes that many of the spirits do not know that they have passed, so they remain lingering.

Former owner Chrisine Burkhart asked Western New York Paranormal to investigate some of the unexplained phenomenon that her son was experiencing on the second floor of the building, an area normally not accessible to patrons. The team recorded an EVP in one of the bedrooms at 147 MHz, a level not audible to the human ear, of a voice saying the words "wake up." The bedroom was her son Zach's former bedroom. Using dowsing rods, the team determined that there was a child spirit still remaining on the second floor of the building. A spirit that was stuck in limbo between worlds. Burkhart explained to the team that it was here in this room that she and her son had experienced voices from the darkness. It happened several times over many, many nights, a voice calling their names. Zach would even be woken up in the middle of the night with his bed being shaken—hearing the words "wake up."

The evening of the investigation, *R-News* reporter Mike O'Brien worked with the diving rods to question the spirit. He asked, "Are you a little boy?" The rods crossed signaling *yes*. He asks, "Are your mom and dad here with you?" The rods part signaling *no*. He continues to ask, "Were you playing with Zack?" and the rods cross again responding *yes*. "Did you like Zack?" *Yes*, the rods respond. "Do you wish Zack was back here with you?" *Yes*, the spirit responds. O'Brien then encourages the child spirit to go to the light and cross over. The rods respond...*Yes*. The rods then completely crossed and gave O'Brien a hug. Sometimes spirits who are lost are scared in death just as they may have been in life. Encouraging them to go to the light because their loved ones await on the other side is all that is needed to cross them over.

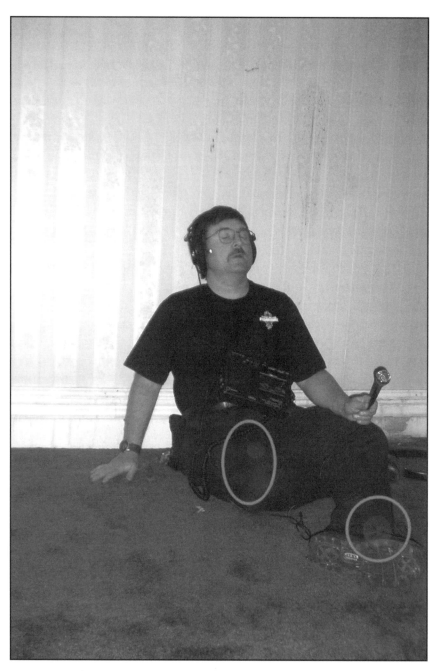

Investigator Paul Heglund, as he "tunes" into the spirit in Zack's room. Notice the spirit orb at his feet.

Edward Harris House
35 Argyle Street
Rochester, New York
www.edwardharrishouse.com

This quaint, nineteenth-century bed and breakfast tucked away in the arts and cultural district of Rochester is home to a spirit affectionately known as "the Captain." So named by the local innkeepers, the Captain is believed to be a long-term resident of the home which was built in 1896. Although he was not a prior resident in the house, it is believed that he was a frequent guest of the family. As the story goes, he often visited the family during his shore leave, while his ship traveled through the Great Lakes region, and was fond of the servants who worked in the home. It's not believed that he died in the home, rather that he was so fond of the family and his memories of his time there that he returns to it often.

According to the innkeepers, it's not unusual to have made the bed in room number three, only to walk past the bed and notice the imprint of someone sitting on it and the smell of freshly- cut flowers. In room number four, guests have smelled the scent of a cigar during their stay and some have felt a strong presence looking over them, as if watching to see what purpose the visitors have in the home. There is definitely nothing to fear in this beautiful bed and breakfast, although there may be mischief afoot. Silverware has been known to disappear from the table, the treadmill in the exercise room has been known to turn on without any power connected, and some have seen the spirit of a young servant running between the rooms on the second floor as if playing a game of ghostly Marco Polo.

It was in October 2005 that Western New York Paranormal, along with a local radio station, conducted an investigation of the bed and breakfast. During the initial investigation, the only anomalies that were discovered were a few spirit orbs and one very weak EVP asking for "help." A few months later, Western New York Paranormal returned to the bed and breakfast to continue the investigation. This time they brought a psychic investigator with them to see if they could pick up on the spirits in the home. This investigation proved to be much more interesting.

The investigation proceeded on the second floor of the establishment, and as the researchers moved from room to room, they noted that a shadow figure would be seen just at the brink of their vision, darting from one room to the next. Then there were two figures. Footsteps were heard running while no one else was on the floor. The psychic investigator felt that a residual haunting might be occurring—a game of hide and seek by two young women wearing nineteenth- century clothing. He felt they may have been servants of the house, one whose name was Emily and the other Clarisse. As one shadow was seen darting into room number three, two members of the team followed, only to discover for themselves the scent of flowers and the imprint of someone sitting on a newly made bed. One investigator's hand passed over the imprint in the bed and a deep drop in temperature was felt, a sign of a potential paranormal presence.

As two investigators worked on the second floor, the remainder of the team walked through the basement. Walking through, they came across a storage area that is normally off limits to guests. A strange presence was felt in the room. The psychic investigator here began to reach out to the spirit—a spirit who seemed to be hiding in a corner of the room. The spirit wouldn't communicate much, other than by giving the impression that it was scared. The psychic sensed the spirit was that of a runaway slave, known to pass through the area on the way to freedom. The spirit seemed confused and not certain of why the researchers were there. It was believed that the spirit hadn't know of its own passing. When asked what year it was for the spirit, it replied, "1930," to the psychic. Later, upon review of audio tape, a low, strained EVP was discovered saying "1930." Unfortunately, the spirit still remains there today, and will until it is ready to move on. As the team began to leave the basement, they noticed that the treadmill they had passed on their way through initially, once off, was now turned on. Turned on, the lights running—but the cord was not plugged into the wall.

What of "the Captain?" Did he make an appearance that evening for the team of Western New York Paranormal? Well he certainly did, in room number four. While four investigators were in the room attempting to communicate with the spirit of the Captain, the temperature in the room dropped ten degrees as the psychic pushed for more communication. Then he could see the spirit. In the mind's eye of the psychic, the spirit appeared to be a tall, strapping gentleman of around six feet tall, maybe a little taller. He had dark hair with a darker complexion and was possibly of Polynesian descent. He couldn't make out the eyes of the spirit because they seemed dark and sunken, but he was wearing a uniform much older than that of World War II. The uniform was a dark blue resembling an older Navy or Merchant Marines uniform bearing a single silver stripe on each shoulder. A single stripe represents the rank of Lieutenant, not Captain. Perhaps in death, spirits are given promotion—or perhaps this one seeks a greater respect in death than he may have received in life.

Wanting more information, the psychic continued to push for information. The dogs on the first floor began barking loudly, over and over again. The voice of the owners could be heard trying to calm the dogs, but to no avail. They sensed something. The psychic began to complain of his eye stinging, perhaps just because of the psychic pressure he was exerting on himself. Nevertheless, he continued to push. He pushed until he was dropped to his knees by someone putting their hands on his shoulders and pushing him down to the floor. The psychic left the building, not to return.

The next day, the psychic awoke suddenly when he heard a voice call to him, "wie sind Sie Prüfer? Es ist verboten." Confused, he went to the bathroom, glanced up into the mirror, catching a glimpse of himself. The eye that had been sore the night before was a now a blackened eye. Was it caused by the pressure he was putting upon himself, or was it a message from the entity? The phrase the investigator heard was German. Translated it meant, "How are you inspector? It's forbidden."

This is the only reported case of "the Captain" ever being forceful with someone in the home. He seems to take pride in protecting what there, both people and items. As with any spirit, treat them with respect and respect is what you will get back most of the time.

In fact, in 2006 the innkeepers sent a photograph to Western New York Paranormal. The photograph was of a young exchange student who came form the Philippines to stay for the summer. As she posed for a picture in front of the main doors prior to leaving, the Captain made an appearance in the photograph. In one of the windows, just right of the main doors there is a face peering out. The face of a distinguished bearded gentleman known as "the Captain."

7

PARKS AND POLTERGEISTS

There is more at play in the parks of Rochester than just children, for many of these parks hold the key to a history passed. A history filled with trauma and turmoil as well as growth and prosperity. Many people don't stop to realize what may have lay on these lands before they were landscaped into what they are today. Although beautiful and breathtaking as each have become, one has to wonder how these parks look to the spirits still lingering from the otherside.

Highland Park
(Sunken Gardens)
South Goodman and Highland Avenue
Rochester, New York

The Sunken Gardens are on the grounds of the historic Warner Castle inside of Highland Park. Warner Castle was designed by by Horatio Gates Warner as a private residence for his family and was completed in 1854. The castle was sold to Frank and Merry Ackerman Dennis, owners of the Dennis Candy Factory and candy stores in 1912. They commissioned landscape architect Alling Stephen DeForest to design gardens for the site beginning around 1920, which

A nighttime view of the Sunken Gardens when spirits come out to play.
Photograph by David Gambino of Penfield, New York.

were completed in 1930. Frank Dennis passed away in 1927, but his wife, Merry, continued to reside in the castle until her death in 1936. The castle remained empty until 1944, when it was purchased from estate by Chrisopher Gainer, a self-styled naturopath, who converted the building into a sanitarium. But with any type of sanatorium, we tend to wonder about the treatment of the individuals who were residents of the facility. At that time in history, it was not uncommon for the residents of such a home to bury their dead on the property in unmarked graves. Family members were rarely present for the deaths nor did they take responsibility. So, are there unmarked graves still present on the property? In was in 1951, when the city of Rochester took over the building and made the residence park of the now Highland Park.

There have been reports of shadow figures moving among the grounds late at night, of items being moved by unexplained means within the castle itself, and unexplained noises. Investigators have made note of recorded EVP and of experiencing areas of fluctuating EMF readings in this region of the park. It is believed that EMF levels will fluctuate in areas of paranormal activity due to the nature of a ghost or spirit being made of energy. There has even been one individual that tells of the sighting of a partially-formed apparition within one of the buildings itself. Rumors have it there used to be an entrance to a series of underground catacombs under Highland Park and into the nearby Mount Hope Cemetery. According to local lore, these are remnants of a long-ago mining operation. There is no official record of these catacombs.

Western New York Paranormal conducted an informal investigation of the grounds at Highland Park in the summer of 2006 with some very interesting results. Although no electronic voice phenomenon were received during the investigation, there were several interesting psychic impressions gathered, as well as photographs. One of the more interesting photographs was taken by investigator David Gambino. This photograph was taken from an overlook of the Sunken Gardens. The spirits of those passed from the Castle still remain.

Highland Park
(Poor House)
Mount Hope Avenue and Highland Avenue
Rochester, New York

In 1836, the Monroe County Poor House was built in the northern section of what is now known as Highland Park. When built, there were three large four-story buildings in place, connected to a farm of over 132 acres. Two basements were occupied with cells for the mentally insane with sitting and sleeping quarters. Individuals were placed eight to a room and there were approximately 280 inmates, including adults and children. These inmates were overseen by one keeper and an assistant. It wasn't unusual for able-bodied paupers to help in care as well. Due to the construction of the house, there was not proper division of the "lunatics" from the general population so there was mistreatment and improper care. As with any poor house of the time, unmarked cemeteries were provided near the buildings as a means of burial for those who could not afford it. The cemeteries were used until 1863. Monroe County took over the property in 1891.

In July 1984, while moving land for a Highland Park addition, a bulldozer unearthed some human remains near the southeast corner of Highland and South Avenues. Investigation proved that these were very old burials. It is thought that these were burials from the poorhouse. It is not certain, but none of the names of those that died in the poorhouse show up in records of any other cemetery. Besides, the burials were not marked and the people were buried in the simplest of wooden coffins. All together, there were 305 remains exhumed from the site, yet many more are still buried on the original site. It is speculated that there are a total of 1,000 burials in the original cemetery.

Many claim to have seen shadow figures wandering the grounds late at night, mysterious orbs of light appearing from nowhere, and eerie mists. There is a general feeling of sadness in this area—a feeling of hopelessness that doesn't belong in such a beautiful park.

Highland Park
(The Lambert Conservatory and Greenhouse)
Reservoir Road
Rochester, New York

Fredreck Law Olmstead was the revolutionary designer behind the city park systems in Rochester, New York. In fact, he helped to make Highland Park one of the first municipal parks in the nation around 1858. In 1911, a conservatory was built on the grounds in honor of a past president of the conservation board, Alexander B. Lamberton. It is today one of the few remaining original buildings in the park. This building has long been the source of many stories of paranormal activity within the park.

Park maintenance worker Roger LeBeau explains that many people have heard voices, footsteps, and even seem figures moving in and around this area. Being inquisitive of the paranormal himself, LeBeau decided to place a tape recorder in the basement of the conservatory among the bulbs, potted plants, and antiques one day when the grounds were closed. As he was placing the recorder, he could hear the sounds of men talking, sounding like they were playing cards. But upon further investigation of the area, Lebeau was alone. He returned an hour or so later to retrieve the tape recorder, and to his amazement, discovered several pieces of electronic voice phenomenon on the recorder. There was an older woman, who sounded like she may have been in her late 70s saying, "HAVE HIM KILLED," with two children, a few moments later, speaking. A small boy, sounding around ten years old said, "IS HE HERE TO HURT US?" with what may have been his older sister, perhaps around twelve, replying, "SHHHHH BE QUIET." Were these spirits of family who may have visited the park or who perhaps wandered from the old sanatorium? No one knows for certain.

An area just behind the Lambert Conservatory, near the line of trees, was the site of a terrible finding in 2003. According to LeBeau, one of park employees stumbled across the body of someone hanging from one of the trees. He tells of a photograph that was taken of the area then showed mysterious orbs and other unexplained phenomenon. To this day, LeBeau can't go near that place without feeling a heaviness come over him, like someone is trying to have their voice heard.

The spirit of the hung or just a phenomenon of the weather?

Ellison Park
(Lost City of Tryon)
395 Rich's Dugway
Rochester, New York

The lost city of Tryon isn't really lost. In fact, thousands of individuals discover it every summer in Penfield. The lost city of Tryon became Monroe County's first county park in December of 1926: Ellison Park.

The City of Tryon was established in 1797. It was located on a well-traveled fur trading route that the French had established as well as a route used by the Native Americans of the region. It was hoped that the city would flourish, but it was soon outpaced by Rochesterville (now the city of Rochester). The City of Tryon was abandoned in the physical since in 1818, but many of its spiritual inhabitants still remain.

Ghost hunters and paranormal enthusiasts find the park still holds much mystery and still holds on to the memories of past residents. Many groups have investigated the lost city, often to fluctuating EMF readings in areas where there should be none. During paranormal investigations, it is believed that spiritual energy can be measured with devices known as tri-field meters or EMF meters. These meters measure fluctuations in the electromagnetic spectrum on the broadband of electrical, magnetic, and direct voltage. It is believed that when spikes or fluctuations occur with no explainable reason for the disturbance that paranormal activity may be occurring.

These fluctuations are quite common among the pine trees at the park, an area devoid of any technology that may influence the meters. Investigators have also captured spiritual orbs on photographs and one evening investigators of RE Paranormal captured a moving, orb-like object darting in and around an investigator.

8

SPOOKED CELEBRITIES

"Everyone has fifteen minutes of fame in their life." Andy Warhol probably didn't take into consideration how fame can be immortal, especially in a city like Rochester where fame reaches beyond death. In her history, Rochester has had its share of the famous and infamous, from greats like George Eastman of Kodak, Susan B. Anthony, Frederick Douglas, and even the notorious Jack the Ripper. There have even been some greats that have passed away in Rochester, although not born here. Among those is screenwriter Rod Sterling. Even in death, the immortally famous continue to make their presence known—in a way that can only happen in Rochester.

Frederick Douglas
Hamilton Street
Rochester, New York

In 1847, Frederick Douglas purchased a two-story home for his family and began his second career in Rochester, New York, as the publisher of the anti-slavery newspaper, *The North Star*. Many people in the Rochester area were not happy with the addition of another anti-slavery newspaper, as well as from other areas of the North. In fact, reports tell that the publisher of the *New York Herald* urged Rochesterarians to dump Douglas' presses into Lake Ontario. But instead, gradually the population of Rochester took pride in the *North Star*, allowing Douglas to become one of the most prominent anti-slavery publishers in the nation. As a result, he became a driving force in the underground railroad. It wasn't unusual for him to show up at work to find runaway slaves sitting on the steps of the newspaper office. It's also said that he would have up to eleven runaway slaves hiding in his home at any given time. It was 1872 when Douglas left Rochester after his home was burned down, losing all records of the *North Star*. He always considered Rochester his home; it was upon his death that he was returned to Mount Hope Cemetery to rest.

In the fall of 2003, Rochester Historian Jean Czerkas knocked on the door on Hamilton Street in Rochester. She had discovered that the home purchased in 1983 by Lee and Sherrie Dukes was once owned by Frederick Douglas. Douglas owned several properties in Rochester, but this is the only one known left surviving. He spent several of his years in this home with his daughter, Rosetta Douglass Sprague.

The owner and husband, Lee, a janitor, was relieved to hear this story. As it turns out, in 1983, he began to encounter the spirit of a black gentleman in the corner of their bedroom. He described him as a very studious black man with gray hair and a top hat. He was always with his head down, always writing and flipping through pages. Intrigued by the story, Czerkas showed the picture of Douglas to Lee who verified him as the man he'd seen so many times. According to an *Associated Press* article, since then, Lee Dukes died of a stroke at age fifty-one. His wife, a breast cancer survivor, recently retired on disability after twenty-three years of working on an assembly line. Both their children, Lewanda and Lee Jr., still live in the home.

White Lady's Castle
Durand Eastman Park
1200 Kings Highway
Rochester, New York

There are various versions of the White Lady Legend of Durand Eastman Park. The most popular version surrounds a woman and her daughter in the late 1800s who had a home near the shore of Lake Ontario. Story tells that, one evening, the daughter disappeared from her bed. The mother, convinced that she was raped and murdered by a local farmer, went out to look for her daughter with her two white German Shepard dogs. The mother searched the marshy swamps near the lake shore where Durand Eastman Park now stands, but no avail. She never found her daughter's body and, in grief, committed suicide. It's said by locals that even after death, on dark, foggy nights, the White Lady rises from the lake with her dogs.

One report, which dates back to 1977, tells of a woman who would routinely cross country ski the golf course at Durand Eastman Park. One gray afternoon she was skiing down the seventeenth fairway and suddenly a cold chill came across her. She turned to notice a woman dressed in a long grayish white coat; with her were two large German Sheppard dogs. Only fifty yards away, she continued to watch the woman until she turned and began to walk towards the shoreline. Although many people walk their dogs in this area, could this have been the White Lady or just another story?

Now if you ask Patricia Wagner, local historian for the *Irondequoit,* she smiles and chuckles a bit at the legend. She tells that there are actually several variations of the legend of the Lady in White—not only along Durand Eastman Park but across the world. She believes the stories to only be folklore and urban legend that have been passed down through the decades, and jokingly said that it was a story to keep young kids away from the shoreline on their dates. She wonders whether, when she walks outside of her front door some foggy spring night, she won't meet a Lady in White who says to her, "What do you mean, I'm not real?"

Haunting of Sam Patch
High Falls District
Rochester, New York
www.centerathighfalls.org

Just like Niagara Falls has had its share of daredevils, Rochester, New York, is no different. They had a gentleman with the name Sam Patch. Patch was a nineteenth-century daredevil born in Pawtuckett, Rhode Island, in 1807. He worked as a child at a local textile mill where he began his daredevil career during his breaks from work. He would entertain the other laborers by jumping off the mill works into the river below. It wasn't long before his jumps drew the attention of local media and grew into well-advertised events, drawing hundreds of people. He quickly moved from jumping off the mill dam to higher locations including waterfalls and bridges. But it was when he was only in his mid-twenties did Patch become known as one of Niagara Fall's first daredevils.

In 1827, according to *American Heritage Magazine*, Patch was invited to jump over Niagara Falls as an added attraction when the local town was blasting an area of the falls known as Table Rock. Table Rock was a large shelf of rock that jutted out over Niagara Falls from the Canadian side. As the horseshoe falls receded, it was noticed in the early 1700s and served as the first vantage point for to the falls for tourists until the early 1800s. For safety purposes, the government planned to blast away part of the shelf after a rock collapse that sent a carriage and its occupants plummeting to their deaths at the falls.

Patch was invited to perform at this event but missed the appointed day. Although late, Patch still found the stunt very inviting, so on Saturday October 17, 1827, a crowd gathered at Goat Island and across the Niagara River in Canada to watch the amazing stunt. On the appointed day it was pouring rain, but Patch boldly climbed a ladder to the platform, which had been built from four trees spliced together and fastened by ropes running back upon Goat Island. With a kiss to the American flag before ascending, he shed his shoes and coat and tied a handkerchief about his neck. Ignoring tearful farewells and protestations from persons at the foot of the ladder, he mounted the narrow, swaying platform which was barely large enough for a man to sit upon, Patch dived into the swirling hood of Niagara Falls. A moment of silence fell over the crowd broken by a joyous celebration when Patch surfaced from the waters. His next challenge was to be Genesee Falls in Rochester, New York.

Patch, by this time, had gathered a strong national following, as well as sponsors, urging him on to higher, more dangerous stunts. In Rochester, a twenty-five-foot scaffolding was erected at the brink of the falls to increase the jump to 125 feet. It was Friday, November 13, 1829, and just over 8,000 people gathered around the falls to watch the death-defying feat. While on his tour in Buffalo, Patch had acquired a pet bear cub which he would now hurl into the waters before any jump that he took. This jump was no different. Poised on the scaffolding, Patch raised his pet above his head and hurled it into the waters below the Genesee Falls. Patch quickly followed. Reports say that about half way through the descent, Patch lost the proper dive posture and a loud splat was heard at the base of the falls. Patch never resurfaced.

Some believed that during the one practice jump Patch had made at the falls, that he had discovered the small cave that lies behind the falls. It was there that he had stored dry clothes, some food, and a bottle of alcohol for plans to later appear. Others believe that he had used "the spirits" to calm his nerves too much before the jump and attempted the feat drunk.

It wasn't until March 17, 1830 that a body was found by a local farmer where the Genesee River empties into Lake Ontario. It was believed to be the body of Patch. As for the pet bear, no one really knows what happened to it. Some reported seeing the bear inside taverns and others claimed that John Sears, a local barber, killed it and made bear grease out of it, according to Rochester Historian Ruth Rosenberg-Naparsteck.

To this day, there have been reports of individuals seeing a figure diving into the falls on that same fate filled November day. Perhaps an entity replaying its last greatest moment. A residual haunting such as this is not unusual when there is so much energy surrounding the original event. In many ways, it records the event, and replays, like an old movie over and over again until the film finally degrades.

On occasion, there have also still been reports of bear sightings in the gorge area. Bears have migrated into the Rochester area over the years in search of new food supplies and to avoid the expansion of man, so it wouldn't be unheard of for a bear to actually exist in the gorge. But who is to say this isn't the pet bear looking for his master?

As for the cave behind the falls, it does exist. In fact, reports have said that should you venture into the cave, you can find it riddled with graffiti, but also laden with melted candles and various symbols marked on the ground and walls. Signs of magic and a suggestion that maybe some people believe that Patch still exists there today.

9

PERSONAL SPOOKS

E very city has their local lore and legends but the truly eerie stories come from the streets themselves. They come from the individuals who aren't out there searching for the ghostly phantoms of the city. They come from those individuals simply living their everyday lives, expecting nothing unusual to happen. But then suddenly, one day, it does. Their lives change forever from that point on, and to that we say: Welcome to haunted Rochester.

"Old Jim"
Abandoned Textile Mill
Henrietta, New York

Thomas Baker of Rochester, New York, accounts an experience that he had in January 2008 with a fellow paranormal enthusiast student of the Rochester Institute of Technology.

Baker had heard the story of a man who was killed in an old warehouse in Rochester, New York. As the story goes, the spirit of this gentleman haunts the warehouse as he still attempts to work on the old stock floor. He is known as "Old Jim," a man to this day trying to work the old abandoned lifts and organize the shelves, not recognizing his purgatory state. There have been several witnesses stating that, when they've been in the building, they feel cold air rushing by them at odd times, sometimes hearing the rustling of shelves and machinery. No witness to date possesses a picture of Old Jim, which is why a local paranormal investigator decided to finally get photographic evidence. Possessing nothing more than a Verizon Venus Camera phone and its night shot function, together they sought the famous old ghost that haunted the warehouse.

On the night of January 24, 2008, they went to the stock floor in search of Old Jim. They heard a few sounds, but nothing out of the ordinary. Suddenly, there was a chilling wind that rushed by them. The investigator felt the breeze as well and looked at Baker, asking if he had felt it, too. Affirming that he had, Baker looked up to notice the stock floor's door swaying ever so slightly. He snapped a picture at that moment of the door. Seeing nothing, he was disappointed, thinking he had missed Old Jim. But when reviewing the picture moments later, there it was, clear as day: a white streak in mid air, going through the open space of the door. It was amazing, and they couldn't believe they were the first to finally get a picture of this famous local resident of the town. A copy of this image can be seen by visiting the gallery section for Haunted Rochester at www.wnyparanormal.org.

WDKX Radio
683 Main Street East
Rochester, New York
www.wdkx.com

The next time you're traveling down that old, haunted highway, turn on your radio to 103.9 FM WDKX, because there may just be a phantom reaching out for its fifteen minutes of fame on late-night radio at local radio station WDKX in downtown Rochester. In October of 2007, one of the local personalities spoke about some of the stories and experiences that have happened in the studios throughout the years.

There are stories of jocks watching shadowy figures walk by their on-air window while working their shifts, many times late at night when no one else is in the building. Apparently the radio station was originally a funeral home and the foundation itself was built on top of an old graveyard-according to local lore. In fact the secretary's office was once an old embalming room, and it would be where she have a haunting experience. It was late one night and she was working on monthly billing for the radio station. She glanced around to notice that she wasn't the only one working late that night. She had noticed someone walk around the corner into her office, and she went to see who it was but no one was there. Someone was definitely working late, however, because she heard the sound of a printer working. Suddenly, she realized it was the calculator on her desk. As she walked closer she witnessed it's keys being punched in one by one, and then the paper tallying. Even the dead work the midnight shift it seems.

Crest Manor Nursing Home
6745 Pittsford-Palmyra Road
Fairport, New York

Every home has its unexplained phenomenon. This is also true for nursing homes—they certainly have plenty of stories that are common among them. For instance, when working around the older population, death is a natural progression of any stay, and as a result, many times staff members grow to have their own superstitions such as opening up the windows of the room to "air the room out" or perhaps to release the spirit. Other times, rooms are left vacant for a few days to prepare for another resident. It provides a good opportunity to clear the energies in the room, but mainly homes report that late at night the "request help" buzzer will often go off in these rooms, even though the rooms are completely vacant. Perhaps mechanical malfunctions or just residual energies from the individual who last occupied that room. You decide.

What makes the Crest Manor Nursing Home interesting is not the ghost stories that it may have, but its live furry mascot. Crest Manor has their own resident cat who is known as the fur reaper. The cat seems to have an uncanny knack for predicting when nursing home patients are going to die, by curling up next to them during their final hours. He is even known to remain outside the room in the days after, just staring into the room, perhaps waiting for the spirit to completely pass on.

The staff and family really don't make a big deal of the furry feline. Research has shown an incredible ability for animals to sense even the smallest of changes in an individual. According to BBC News, tales have long existed of dogs detecting various types of cancer with their sense of smell. A study later proved that dogs could sense evidence of bladder cancer by smelling it in urine. Some people who suffer from serious epilepsy use specially-trained dogs provided by charities. These dogs warn their owners of impending seizures by licking or some other signal. One woman said that her dog regularly gives her a forty-minute warning, allowing her to get to a safe place so as not to worry about the seizures putting her in danger. This doesn't explain the talent of the Crest Manor feline, but but he does provide a very comforting aspect of hospice.

Demon in the Mirror
Greece, New York

It all began when this young girl was six years old. She lived in a home on the west side of Rochester near Culver Avenue. There was nothing really fancy about the home, but it did have an interesting history. It seems the home her family lived in was at one time a funeral home. It had since been converted into apartments. The mother and daughter lived there with the mother's boyfriend. For quite some time it seemed like any other home. Any other home that is until the boyfriend began to see shadows moving out of the corner of his eye. He also began to hear footsteps inside the home. It wasn't long after, the boyfriend ran across a woman in the residence. He described her as having long, curly-blond hair and as very attractive. When he turned to tell the girlfriend that one of her friends was there, because he didn't know who it was, the woman vanished. Sightings of the woman became more frequent in the home, but it wasn't just the boyfriend seeing her. The young daughter was also seeing the apparition and it scared her.

It was past midnight one night when the boyfriend felt someone rubbing his cheek gently and an arm caressing down his side. He thought it was his girlfriend until he opened his eyes. It was the spirit of the woman, who began to transform before his eyes. He felt paralyzed and was held down in bed. He struggled and tried to call out but his girlfriend didn't respond. It was as if she was in a deep state of *unraisable* sleep.

The boyfriend had an encounter with a succubus. A succubus is a demon who takes the form of a beautiful woman in order to seduce a male for sexual intercourse. They draw energy from men to sustain themselves. After this encounter, things began to change in the household.

The energy in the home changed from one of happiness to one of discomfort and irrational behavior. Arguments would spur out of nowhere and, at times, confrontations would become physical. Depression became commonplace in the home. A paranormal team was called in to investigate the unusual phenomenon. They set up several cameras throughout the residence and began their investigation. The team psychic sensed that the entity there intended to cause great harm to the family and it was somehow attached to the mother's family. The family was warned that the child should be carefully watched because she was very open to the spiritual world and could be a magnet to entities. As they ended their investigation, the team leader was upstairs packing his equipment. The investigator standing next to him was flung into the nearby closet like a child had thrown a rag doll. The investigator who was thrown was a very large gentleman, approximately six foot tall, around 250 pounds, not an easy person to push around. After this event the team was very shaken. They packed up quickly and left the home and the investigators were never heard from again.

It was ten years later that Western New York Paranormal received a telephone call from the mother. She told the story of the past encounter and how shortly after that incident, she and her daughter had moved from place to place. Recently, they had settled in a small apartment in Greece and things were getting bad. She was scared for her safety and the life of her daughter.

In the past thirteen years, both she and her daughter had become seriously ill. Both had multiple medical conditions that seemed to appear out of nowhere. They were having extreme runs of bad luck and now they were being terrorized in their home by several unseen entities. Entities that would fling cupboard doors open and shut. Something would cause the foulest stenches to move through the home, smelling like rotting flesh and death itself. They would hear growls and snarls from the basement and from within the daughter's upstairs closet. Both had been physically assaulted in the home and reported being hit by unseen forces with the mother suffering from physical slashes manifesting and causing blood to run.

In an effort to protect herself, the daughter had turned to witchcraft. She wrote spells of protection around the frame of her bedroom door and over her windows. She had made a crystal wand and began casting spells in an attempt to protect herself, but it was to no avail. On one such occasion, she was trying to invoke a spell of protection only to have the entity which had been plaguing the family appear to her in the mirror in her bedroom. It terrified her. This is when the mother called Western New York Paranormal.

Initially, the team went to speak with the mother and daughter. As the team arrived at the home, the lead investigator sat with the mother and daughter discussing in full detail what had occurred within the home, along with their longer history of their family's haunting. This allowed two other team members to conduct an initial investigation or walk through of the home taking pictures and recording test EVP to get an overall feel for the home. The conversation was mostly between the lead investigator and the mother, the daughter seemed very distrustful and cautious, which was understandable for all that she had gone through.

Walking through the house felt much like walking through quicksand. Lead investigator had brought a psychic investigator from Monroe County Paranormal Investigations to walk through the home who knew nothing at all of the case. This is common practice in paranormal investigations so that those impressions received by individuals are not tainted with any knowledge they may have had regarding the case. The home felt like an energy sink; the investigators who walked the halls and through the rooms could feel it drain their energy.

After the walk through of the home, the lead investigator joined Rob, who was the psychic investigator on site from Monroe County Paranormal Investigations, in a separate walkthrough of the property to hear some of his impressions. They first went to the daughter's room where Rob spoke of an entity there that wouldn't allow itself to be seen. As Rob stood in the bedroom, he could look into a mirror over the dresser and see an entity standing behind him. Every time Rob moved to see the entity, the entity would hide behind him again—playing a game of cat and mouse. He explained that he really couldn't get a read of what it was and only knew that the reason it was there was because it was *called* there by the daughter. She had opened the doorway for it to enter the life of the family. When it was asked how it entered into their lives, it replied, "Through the door, and not all doorways are outside." Of course, it was referring to a doorway that the daughter had opened up within herself somehow. The entity began to become verbally aggressive with Rob, who then began to feel short of breath. It was apparent that the being did not want the investigators there.

While the two investigators were upstairs, the team (who was now with the family) began to hear noises from the basement. The sounds were that of items being thrown. Investigators headed to the basement only to discover a very orderly basement with nothing out of place. There was no evidence of anything being thrown. The only thing out of place was the smell. A foul smell whose origin could not be identified. It could only be described as a mixture of rotting flesh and feces. The team understood that there was definitely something serious going on in this home. So lead investigator explained to the family that they would be in touch shortly. The plan would be to provide the family with some form of spiritual protection and to conduct a blessing of the home.

One investigator that evening, Stacie, had noticed a small "post it" note on a shelf in the daughter's room. The note said the lead investigator's name with a physical description of him and the words spiritually powerful. The daughter knew nothing of investigator until he knocked at the door of the home. The mother hadn't told her of him.

It was a day later that he received an e-mail from Monroe County Paranormal Investigations. In the e-mail was a photograph that was taken in the daughter's room. It was the entity that had been playing cat and mouse with Rob that night—a demon reflecting back in the mirror. A face that resembled what the grim reaper may look like to many. It had sunken eyes, skull-like features and fanged teeth. It was horrifying. This coupled with an EVP recording that Dwayne had captured in the daughter's room that evening with Rob, hissing and saying "get out" only served to reinforce the fact that the family was in danger.

Cleansing a home is a matter of faith. Not just the power of faith of the individual conducting the blessing, but also faith of the individuals in the home and belief in the power of prayer. Since this family had mixed spiritual beliefs, Dwayne called on a group of local Wiccans to assist his team in cleansing the home. The power of prayer and faith would be coming from a side of Christianity and that of Wicca reaching into the beliefs of everyone in the home.

An eerie calm came over the home the evening the group was scheduled to arrive. All the unexplained activity that had

A demon in the mirror.
Photograph by Kathlene Pastilli, Monroe County Paranormal Investigators.

run so rampant came to a halt. The mood in the house was light and happy. The family questioned if they really needed to do a blessing since the activity seemed to stop on its own. They believed that the paranormal mayhem was gone. It was suggested the family still do the blessing of the home.

It's common for one of two events to occur before a blessing of a home. The paranormal activity in the home can dramatically increase. It can escalate in the form of a threat against the individuals in the home as a warning for them not to meddle with the situation at hand or things might get worse. Or, homes can also become very quiet, very "normal." The entities at play often will go into hiding in an act of trickery. The entities attempt to fool the family into thinking that they have left the home and all is right with the world. Many times, what happens is the activity only begins over again, shortly afterwards. Oftentimes, in either spiritual strategy, the activity escalates much quicker after the deception. Understanding this, the family agreed to continue with the blessing.

Beginning in the basement, the group of prayer warriors worked using a combination of traditional Christian prayer and blessing with holy water combined with technique of "toning" which was used by the Wiccan group. Toning is a technique where individuals use certain sound vibrations to, in effect, raise the energy level of a home, not allowing for lower forms of energy or entities to remain; whereas a blessing uses faith and prayer to call upon God to fill the home with the light of Heaven and as needed send the angels for assistance. As they worked in the basement, the psychics present could "feel" areas in the basement where the energy were the strongest and they seemed to form a triangle flowing from one point to another. Interestingly, if these points were to become pillars that extended up through the home, these would be the areas that were the strongest in the home for paranormal activity.

As the cleansing team came up the stairs from the basement, the daughter gave a look of distrust and disgust to the team. They entered the kitchen and began their prayers. As they were praying, it was heard from the mother, who was in the living room the words, "Do it now." And when the words were finished, a team member caught a glimpse of the daughter nodding her head gently as she stared into the kitchen. There was a "mechanical" blink that she made as if trying to make something or prevent something from happening. The young girl was attempting to prevent the cleansing prayers from being successful. Realizing this, an investigator moved to block the door so that the daughter would no longer have a clear view of the blessing.

The blessing of the kitchen continued, and as it did, Rob noticed a small child spirit that was in the room. A harmless child that liked to play with the family but was also very scared of what dark entities lurked within the home. As they left the kitchen, the gaze fell upon the lead investigator. It was the gaze of something without a soul and it wasn't this young girl. In fact, it was something much darker. Rob stayed with the girl to talk with her and offer some prayer while the team continued on.

The team brought a light, lifting energy to each room that they entered. They then fell upon the daughter's room. The foul smell of death rose within the room and the team began to pray. As the psychics looked into the dresser mirror, they described what they were seeing as though they were looking through ripples of water. The object wasn't solid by any means, but perhaps was a portal—a portal by which some of the entities in this home had passed through. The daughter in the home told the team that she would ask for protection while gazing into the mirror in her bedroom. This perhaps had opened another doorway into the home.

With a hand lain on the mirror and the other in the air, the lead investigator began to pray. He prayed for God to fill the room with the white light of Heaven and send His angels down to bind the creature that was there. It would be bound to silence and be bound from causing harm to anyone. He prayed for it to be pushed back through the mirror from which it came, closing the doorway behind it. As he said his words, he described feeling energy rush through him like a conduit. It came through the hand he had raised in the air down through him and back into the mirror...moments later, a loud slam was heard. The team called upstairs saying, "You're not going to believe this." The upstairs team walked down stairs to find the cupboard doors all open in the kitchen. No one had been in there. They flew open all on their own. Rob walked in behind the lead investigator with his head bowed and said, "The child spirit here thanks you. He doesn't have to hide anymore. But there is still one more."

In the basement, in the darkest corner, lay in hiding one last entity with a name that was unpronounceable. The lead investigator prayed for the basement to be filled with white light again and that all hiding places be removed bringing forth all that remained. Rob's hand went to his ears as he dropped to one knee. "I have never heard such a horrific shrill in all of my life. It was a scream of agony and then a rush of energy—now it's gone." There is always one left that lingers. It's the most powerful. It is the duty of those entities least powerful to distract away from the leader. In this case, these entities were demonic.

The house had a much lighter, fresh feel to it. It was much like that of a new spring day. As with any cleaning, it's up to the homeowners to keep the home clean. Demonic entities though, like bugs, will often come back to test the waters and test the faith. It's up to the homeowners now to keep that from happening. They were able to witness the power of what each of the faiths could bring. They would now have to keep and build the faith.

Private Residence
Allerton Street
Grecce, New York

About fifteen minutes from downtown Rochester sits a house nestled in a cozy neighborhood called KodaVista, so named due to its proximity to Kodak-one of Rochester's largest industries. This house is one of many in the Rochester area that is flanked by paranormal activity, but what makes it interesting is that none of the activity that once occurred in the home was due to historical events, residual energy, or traumatic happenings. Rather, the activity centered in this home was created due to one specific reason: Its owner was, at the time, an amateur ghost hunter.

A Story Shared by Sarah Claud

I remember very clearly what it was like when I first walked through what would be my new home. It was about as peaceful as any home could be. Sunny windows and a large porch, enough room to breathe, but small enough to still feel cozy, I couldn't imagine a nicer place to begin my new life as an independent woman. When the purchase closed about a month later, I eagerly moved all of my belongings into it along with my young daughter and we began our new life together with little incident.

As time would reveal, however, there were plenty of incidents yet to occur, and not all would remain serene. As 2002 turned into 2003, my interest in ghost hunting grew, and I found myself on more and more paranormal investigations. Being the amateur that I was, I'm not hesitant to admit that I wasn't as spiritually protected as I am now. As a result, things began happening in my home—chilling things that no one should have to experience in their lifetime. Rappings on the walls would occur in the middle of the night. My hair would be pulled, jarring me from peaceful sleep. My name, Sarah, would be yelled—startling me from whatever task I was performing at the time. Objects would vanish and not return, despite my demands that they be returned. Yet none of these pesky annoyances were as concerning as some of the physical attacks that began to occur, that nearly spiraled out of control before I finally moved from the home.

I began to have lucid dreams, the sensation that you are awake in your own dreams. At night, I would have what is called sleep paralysis—waking up to apparitions in my bedroom and having the inability to move or speak to them while they terrified me. I would find random marks on my body, the source of such marks being unknown… and once, during the investigation of a particularly dark haunting, I experienced love bites on my neck that appeared after showering one morning. These marks had again manifested from an unknown source. It was time for everything to stop.

The final straw occurred one morning shortly after waking. I walked into my daughter's bedroom to find her coloring a picture. She looked at me and said, "Mommy, I'm scared." When I asked her why, she told me that at night there were scary faces in her bedroom windows. Her coloring depicted the horrors that were invading her sleep at night, complete with fangs and gaping eyes. The drawing showed her on the bed, covering her face in terror. It was then that it hit me: This had to stop, and stop immediately. No longer could these entities be allowed to plague my home, especially when it seemed that the reason they were infesting my home was due to my immersion in the paranormal. I needed to get protection in place, quickly, and get the home blessed even quicker.

Dwayne is one of the many people I was ghost hunting with at the time. We had become very powerful together on investigations, and eventually would become husband and wife. However, that night, he came to my home armed with holy water and prayers, and I fully believed that we would be able to clear the home of the entities plaguing us for the last few months.

He began in the attic, a large expanse filled with mostly empty boxes and Christmas ornaments. As he began to pray, I began to hear banging and other noises coming from downstairs, a sign that energies were being stirred and that the entities attached to the home were reluctant to go. As I sat on the couch in the living room, I began to see mists floating from one room to the next, and clearly heard the word "NO!" spoken in a low, guttural voice that wasn't Dwayne's. As I sat, I could hear Dwayne moving from one bedroom to the next, systematically blessing the house. As he persisted, things began to feel lighter and lighter. At the conclusion of his blessing, from attic to basement, we decided that while many energies had been cleared from the home, there were still some in hiding, not wanting to pass from the depths of my house to the blissful landscapes of the other side. No, we could not completely call this a successful house cleaning, but for now, things were calmer.

Months went on and many things occurred in my life. My daughter and I were living peacefully in the house with no further problems. I ended up putting the house on the market. The house itself had been oddly quiet, almost as if it knew these were my final days in it, and it came no surprise to us that things began to get active again as we prepared for its sale. As we painted the walls and made minor repairs, the house moaned and creaked. As we carried out boxes and eventually the furniture, the house seemed to howl with loneliness. And as we did a final walkthrough of the place, it was then that we decided to bless the home one last time.

The attic was quiet as we ascended the stairs, feeling the warm rush of heat from the sun pounding in the windows. We looked at each other briefly and then Dwayne began to say prayers of cleansing, praying for any lost souls to finally return to the other side. The house began to feel lighter, and soon after the blessings, we finally left the house forever, leaving it with prayers of a joyous life for its future homeowners and only wonderful energies in the lifetimes to come.

As a ghost hunter, the house taught me many lessons. The most important was to always shroud yourself with appropriate protection while investigating. Entities can easily attach to you, making your home their final resting ground. It then becomes your responsibility to encourage these lost spirits to the other side, helping them to find solace. Perhaps the entities I experienced at the Allerton home were there years, decades, eons before I lived there, but I still felt it my job to help them find their way home.

But I often wonder, have the new residents of the home encountered any of the ghostly entities I experienced while living there? Or have they finally found their way home? I can't be sure, but every time I pass the house, it seems to smile, as if now it has finally found peace.

Big Red Barn
122 Stryker Road
Rochester, New York

From an article written by Carole Daugherty Thoms

The big red barn at 122 Stryker Road has stories to tell. Sitting close to the road, it is a reminder that Stryker Road was once just a farm lane separating the barn and the house. As late as the early 1900s, the road did not yet connect to Stottle Road. The farm passed down through the Grunendike and Striker [Stryker] families who owned the property for much of its 180 years. Other occupants over the years are familiar names in Chili: Laney, Hauslaurer, and Daugherty. Current owner, Carole Daugherty Thoms lives in the home her father was born in. Births, baptisms, weddings, deaths and all the living in between have occurred at 122. The barn, as well as the house, has seen events mark its long history. Used as a dairy barn in the early 1900s with milk bottled

A barn with a haunted history. *Photograph by Carole Daugherty Thoms.*

in the basement of the house, the barn around that same period was changed from a gamble to a straight roof profile. Massive hand hewn-beams and rubble-stone foundation with chiseled initials, give testament to the building's early history. A sign over the former draft horse stalls, displays a draft horse shoe and the words "Horse Style Real Style." For over thirty years the barn also housed champion Morgan Horses and many foals saw the first light of day in the big roomy foaling stall filled with golden straw and walled on one side with rubble stone. The bank barn, a traditional German construction technique, sits snugly against a bank of dirt fronting the road, keeping the lower level warm in the winter and cooler in the summer. In recent years, there have been occasional hints of events from the barn's past. Stories passed on tell about a fall from the mow of the barn resulting in a death. It was reported that a voice was heard giving a stern reminder not to drink. A few years ago, while preparing the application for a New York State Barn Preservation Grant, my youngest daughter took an ordinary disposable 35mm camera and shot a roll of film, focusing on areas needing repair, interesting architectural details, and overall views of the barn, with no unusual happenings. Soon after, sitting under the warm glow of the dining room chandelier, the photos were spread across the old table, to choose the proper images to tell the story of the barn. My daughter handed me a shot of a large, hand-hewn beam that spanned the depth of the barn. "How about this one?" she asked, thinking that it showed an interesting architectural detail.

The beam was illuminated by a single bare bulb, directing attention to its massive dimensions and rough texture, or at least it would have directed attention to the beam if it wasn't for a foggy, white specter in the upper left corner; ten feet above the floor, an apparition had materialized into an unmistakable form of a face. Upon further study of the prints, other pictures my daughter had dismissed and set aside, were re-examined. Some of them also showed a dense, thick fog consumed the space. No face this time, but an amorphous shape was not in the viewfinder when the shot was taken. In spite of these happenings, one feels safe and comfortable within the barn walls, as if a haunting approval were there for the continuation of its use and care.

Private Residence
57 Gothic Street
Rochester, New York

From 1963 to 1967, a small family of one sister and two brothers and their father lived in an older home in Rochester, New York. It was a solid two and a half story, three bedroom home built sometime in the 1920s. Even though worn, there were hardwood floors throughout the home. The formal dining room had a huge bay window with a window seat and built-in cabinets on both sides of the window, constructed of gumwood and leaded glass. The chandelier was made of brushed silver with blue highlights and hundreds of oval, beveled crystals that shimmered beautifully in the sunlight. The house had a parlor by the front door and a full pantry off of the very out-dated kitchen. The living room had an entire wall of gumwood and leaded glass cabinets with gumwood trim on ceiling and floor. The family loved the house because it was the first one they could call their own, but the love affair with the house on Gothic Street began to cool off when they all came to realize that the house was truly haunted. It was the summer before the daughter's sixteenth birthday. She loved being alone to paint, write, or just listen to her records. That day she was up in her room writing, and being her age, she craved her privacy. She always kept her door closed whether anyone was home or not because, for some reason, she never felt quite secure in the house. She always had the feeling that she wasn't altogether alone, even in an empty house. She was totally absorbed in her writings when a knocking started on her bedroom door. Fear coiled around her like a noose. It was loud and at first she thought one of her brothers had come home and was trying to scare her. So she got up out of her chair, totally shaken, and went to the door. She held the cool glass doorknob in her hand and then the knocking stopped. Just as she was about to open the door, the knocking started again. Not lightly as before, but pounding, as if someone was beating the door with their fists. She was so afraid that she couldn't breath as terror filled her. She leaned into the door since there was no lock, hoping that who ever was out in the hall wouldn't try to come into her room. The pounding was persistent. She wanted it to stop. She needed it to stop. The awful, ear-shattering noise just kept on. Yet, as she leaned full weight into the door, she felt no vibration through the oak. For a moment, she thought she was losing her mind and started to cry, feeling so alone and vulnerable, and she slid to the floor, As she leaned against the smooth wood, hoping that whatever was on the other side wouldn't try to enter, the pounding stopped. She didn't move. She couldn't move. Her body seemed paralyzed, permeated with fear. Soon after, she heard footsteps on the wooden stairs. Her heart almost burst with anxiety. Imagine her relief when she heard her father's voice and her brothers close behind asking if she had finished her project. She was never so happy to see her brothers and father as she was at that moment. They had not heard a thing when they came into the house, but soon, in time, they would all know the fear that she experienced that night in the house on Gothic Street.

One evening, the family had gone to bed and the father, who shared a bedroom with the brothers, started to hear loud music playing throughout the house. At first, the brothers thought it was their sister playing music in her room. The father began complaining to them about the music and how loudly the daughter always played it. It was then that the daughter came out of her room and stood at the door of the boy's bedroom with a scared look on her face. Her father asked her why she had the radio on so loud and the daughter shook her head no—it was coming from downstairs. The family worked their way downstairs to investigate, with the father leading the way, fear so powerful, they could feel their hearts pounding! The television had been turned on with the volume knob turned up all the way. These were the days before remote controls, It was a television set that had no remote control, only dials and knobs on the set itself that physically had to be turned. Someone or something had physically pulled that knob out to turn the television on and turned the knob to the right several times to set it to full volume. This terrified the entire family because no longer was this just the "story" of a young sixteen-year-old girl, but now an event that the entire family had experienced.

It has been many years since the family has moved away from this house leaving those experiences far behind them. Although no more stories have been told from other tenants of the home, I would have to speculate that this haunting was just getting started and is perhaps now waiting for the just the right family to arrive to begin again.

Private Residence
Henrietta Road
Rochester, New York

The year was 1969; a young student by the name of Bruce Randall had just moved into a small but modest apartment in a home on Henrietta Road. Randall was attending the Rochester

Institute of Technology that year as a student. There had been rumors that this home was haunted. As the story went, a prior tenant who lived in the home had fallen down the stairs, and if you stood on the third step, where the fall began, you could feel a change in temperature. A cold spot is not that uncommon in homes with paranormal activity. Cold spots are caused when spirits begin to pull energy from their surrounding environment to help them manifest. Energy can be drawn from a variety of sources, including electrical outlets and batteries, people themselves, even the air. As kinetic energy is drawn from the surrounding air, it causes the air to cool, thus a cold spot.

Cold spots, however, were not the only unexplained phenomenon that occurred in this home. It was also documented that when individuals sat in the living room, the lights would be turned on and off—on cue. The upstairs shower would turn itself on—all by itself—among many other incidents.

Now, most people would be a bit put off by these stories, but not Randall. He was a very logical gentleman and there was a scientific explanation for everything that could happen. That's what he thought, anyway.

One evening, there was a small gathering at the house when the party games were broke out. One of the games brought by a guest was a Ouija® Board. The small group gathered in a circle in the living room where they began to use the board—asking questions of the supposedly dead tenant. Randall, having had enough of the ghost games, thought he'd put an end to the ghost nonsense once and for all. He was determined to see if all this stuff was real or not, so he headed to the attic where the tenant used to play as a child. As the story was told, she was developmentally challenged and apparently her parents had been ashamed of her and kept her upstairs for most of her life. In searching the attic space, he discovered numerous doll outfits stuck under the floor boards which began to give credence to the story of the tenant at the very least.

He made his way over to an old laundry chute that ended in the attic. The chute extended downward two stories to the basement. In the lore of the home, the deceased was rumored to haunt the home and, more specifically, the laundry chute. As he sat there watching down the chute, the voices from the living room could be heard asking questions. Someone asked the question, "Would you like to play?" and no sooner had the phrase been completed, then Randall noticed a pale blue light in the darkness of the chute. As he watched, the light began to climb up from the bottom of the chute, looking more foggy and misty as it climbed higher and higher until settling about midway up the two-story chute. He took the watch off his wrist and placed it down on a board that crossed the chute and then backed away. Randall asked, "So would you like to play?" He then watched as the blue mist rose from the chute and engulfed the watch. Scared, he turned to leave the attic and began to climb down the ladder. As he lowered himself down the ladder, the door suddenly slammed down onto his hands cutting them both badly. There was no way this door could have closed on its own. It was hinged open at a greater than sixty-degree angle; "Someone" had decided to play rougher than what Randall had expected.

Randall returned to the group in the living room who were still playing with the Ouija® Board. He suggested that the group ask for the ghost of the house to speak to them. He watched as the planchette circled round and around on the board as it spelled out, "What do you want?" He said to it, "If you are truly a ghost and real, tell everyone what just happened." The board began to spell again... "T-i-c T-o-c T-i-c T-o-c H-a H-a H-a H-a" and then the planchette flew across the room hitting the wall over twelve feet away.

Did Randall injury himself or was it just a playful child? Did his friends really know what happened and decided to move the planchette to add to the experience? Whatever it is that really happened, Randall was left having a new respect for the ghost of Henrietta Road.

10

TRAVELLIN' SPIRITS

A ghostly mystery behind every road, phantoms that travel the rails, and creatures of darkness that lurk underneath the city itself. These are certainly stories that are familiar to everyone. They are what urban legends and local folklore are made of. But what if there were an ounce of truth to them? What if behind the lore, there was some fact? What if there was someone, that you knew, who had actually experienced everything that you've ever heard? Would you be more careful how you chose to travel in and around Rochester?

Interstate 90
Between Buffalo and Rochester

A haunting is not limited to just objects and homes. They can also occur on the roadways we travel. There isn't a city without a tale of a haunted highway traveler looking for a ride or flagging passersby for help, only to disappear once they have received the attention they sought. Interstate 90 which runs between Rochester and Buffalo is no different. Jennifer Edmiston recalls one such trip she had on that well-traveled highway.

"Over the years that I have sensed paranormal presences, the way in which I experience phenomena varies with each encounter. Unlike many that consistently experience with the same set of senses every time, mine truly vary. "One of my first naked-eye encounters occurred while driving down a Rochester expressway at about 12:30 at night. I was moving along and as I rounded a bend my headlights shone onto the side of the road, reflecting off the leaves of trees in the distance. And for a brief moment, my lights lit up a man who was standing off the shoulder of the road. He appeared to be standing down the embankment just a bit, and I noted a very clear image of him: dark hair, scruffy face, and a brown leather jacket. But in that brief moment, I also noticed he had blood on his face and was looking right at me. "Of course, I immediately thought he had been in an accident and needed help, and as I started to put on my brakes to stop and help him, his image quickly disappeared. And where I saw the man, suddenly, a cross with flowers on it appeared. Clearly someone had died in an accident on that spot. You can imagine the shock of first seeing someone injured and in need of help, and a flash of a moment later, realizing he wasn't a living person, and then seeing a marker memorializing someone's death. "It is my belief that he appeared as a warning that I was going far too fast around a significant bend in the highway. I believe that I saw him that night for a reason, as a sign. I can still see the man's image in my mind quite clearly. It is still my intent to search records to find out the identity of the person who died at that spot, and see if there is any correlation to his image and that of the person who suffered an untimely fate there. "Needless to say, every time I come to that area, I am reminded… and I slow it down."

The Story of Arthur R. Stillwell
Spirits guided him to build 3,000 miles of railroad track
Rochester, New York

Arthur R. Stillwell was born in September 1876, and shortly thereafter moved to Rochester, New York, with his mother. They rented a modest home on the east side of the city—then known as Rochesterville. It was at the age of four that his mother began to notice the special gifts that her son had. According to an article dated June 15, 1922, Stillwell would commonly warn his mother of relatives who would be coming to visit days before their arrival. Although she greatly discouraged this talent in her son, she often boasted of the gift her son possessed. She referred to it as "second sight." It was at the age of fourteen that Stillwell began to see a girl who no one else could see. He described her as a beautiful, brown-haired woman. She was tall and slender with long curly hair. He told his mother that this was the woman who he would marry when he was nineteen. He stated that he didn't know her name, but that in time, it would be Stillwell. At the age of nineteen, his premonition came true.

Later in life, Stillwell became a railroad engineer by trade. He was monumental in the building of over 3,000 miles of railroad track that connected the east coast to Kansas City. He claimed that he had not only laid more railroad track than any man alive, but that every part of every route was determined by spirits that came to him in dream, telling him where to go. One important section of the railroad route that Stillwell built was the track of Kansas City Southern. Spirits had come to Stillwell, warning him not to build the railroad terminal at Galveston. If he did, it would be disastrous. Spirit had suggested, instead, that the terminal be placed at Lake Sabine. As he did for all those many thousands of miles before, Stillwell followed the guidance of the spirits and terminated the line at what is now called Port Arthur, which is named after him. It was just four days after the terminal was completed that a tidal wave wiped out Galveston. (*New York Times*, 1922)

Stillwell lived many years of his life hiding his secret, fearing people would think he was crazy. For the latter part of his years, however, many of his friends and directors of the companies he worked with, grew to know his inspiration, believing in the spiritual guidance.

In 1922, Stillwell announced to the world the gifts that he had and then began to write. He accomplished several novels through spirit-writing including, *The Court's Decree* and *In God's*

Own Time. He also wrote the words and music to the children's songs "Slumberland" and "Dreamland," while communing with the spirit. It makes you wonder, the next time you have some creative inspiration—could it be from beyond the grave?

New York Central Railway
Richmond Avenue area
Rochester, New York

A lone stretch of railway tracks from an era long passed still remains. People still see the occasional train engine passing through, dragging with it its load of cargo—but on some nights, you may just come across another traveler working his way home.

As local legend says that people have seen a lone individual walking down the railway bed late at night—a wispy figure whistling a tune of merriment, only to seemingly disappear in the late-night mist. As the local newspaper reports from May 1908, Edward Dumphry, who was a well-known man about town and proprietor of the Lockview Hotel, had left his place of business around 1 am on the morning of May 28th. A stranger had come through the area and had asked for a ride to a nearby farm, just west of the city, that he was considering purchasing. Dumphry, being the good man that he was, offered to help the stranger reach the farm. No need to walk the roads that late at night. Who knows what could happen? So they were off. It was around 5 am when the horse and buggy returned to the hotel, without Dumphry. It was later that morning that trainmen from the New York Central Railway found Dumphrey's remains.

Authorities assumed that he had been thrown from his horse and buggy and that he'd attempted to follow the railroad tracks home. Instead of reaching his destination, Dumphry lay in pieces on the railway. The body literally cut apart. His legs and right arm were severed completely off while the trunk of his body was severely cut and bruised. Now his spirit walks the rails, just looking for a way home.

Rochester Subway System
Beneath Broad Street
Rochester, New York

Rochester was one of the smallest cities in the United States to have its own subway system. Built in 1927, the underground transportation system moved passengers east and west underneath Broad Street for more than thirty years. It was after the Erie Canal was re-routed around downtown Rochester in 1919 that Rochester covered the old canal bed with Broad Street. They then laid tracks along the dry canal bed—anticipating a growth in Rochester that never came. The railway made about a dozen stops, each of which linked passengers with other railway systems that could connect people to the rest of New York State. Ridership on the system peaked during the Depression, but came to a screeching halt shortly after World War II when there was an improvement in the economy. People began to purchase their own transportation and the city grew in directions not served by the subway system.

The system was finally shut down in 1956. What remains today is a pipeline of gloom running beneath downtown, nearly two miles of rusted track littered with burned-out ticket stations and the art of graffiti writers. It is a home to the homeless people...and much more. Legends surround the subway system—stories of phantoms who walk the tunnels. It is also said that it is a vampire haven for Rochester. However, to city officials, the old tunnel is a monument to decay, a big pothole just begging to be filled.

Urban explorers describe the open areas of the subway system as stunning, beautifully-filled chambers of water with urban water falls and stone archways, reminiscent of Greek architecture. An amazing city beneath the city, away from the light. It isn't far, though, that an explorer has to walk before they find the tunnels...tunnels that lead into the most pitch-black darkness that someone will ever encounter. The homeless of Rochester are not the only ones living in that darkness.

One exploration of the underground tunnel system was described by an investigator from Canada. Walking down one tunnel, the researcher began to hear a strange noise by the City Hall Station. While walking down the tunnel, the sound became louder and louder. This noise sounded like nothing less fearsome than a zombie-monster dragging its enormous coffin behind it, trailing metal chains along the ground. The investigator stated that the only human thing even conceivable of it being part of real life was a battalion of angry homeless residents hauling heavy trash cans behind them in order to attack to the group—but really that seemed unlikely. Although they searched, they could find no reasonable source for the noise. The pattern itself was far too regular for it to be human. At times the noise sounded like it was ahead of them, at other times behind them or above them. They pressed on until they realized the tunnel dead-ended.

The Paranormal and Ghost Society, formally of Buffalo, performed a small-scale investigation of the tunnel system as well. They discovered many areas of fluctuating EMF readings where they took photographs. In the photographs, mysterious images of faces and mists appeared. One was described as a female with a "punked-out look" to her; another was described with creature-like features. Who knows if these were images that the mind was just trying to make sense of, or if there are actually spirits in the subways? Some have reported seeing phantoms that walk amongst the darkness in the old station areas or they see phantoms that disappear once they cross the old rails. They may just be figments of the imagination or they may be deceased passengers taking a final ride on the spirit express.

Many have died in the tunnels over the decades. Homeless people wander there, never to leave, and the Rochester Police Department has numerous reports of bodies that have been dumped there. It's a place of gloom and darkness. A place that is best left alone and kept as a part of Rochester's folklore.

11

GHOSTLY GALLERIES

They're places of history—galleries that hold treasures that link us to our past. Museums hold much more than artifacts that are hundreds of years old, though. They can hold memories and impressions from the time they represent. Walking into a home that's over 100 years old which has been restored to its splendor can make a visitor feel like they are part of that time and that history. Walking into a museum's gallery can make a person feel the empathy of the history it represents. Who is to say that the same energy can't remain long after those people experiencing it have left? After all, wars have been fought on these lands. Families have lived in these homes. The common thread between them? Passion. A passion that keeps many connected still today.

Genesee County Village
1410 Flint Fill Road
Mumford, New York
www.gcv.org

A rise above the Oatka Creek in a quiet corner of Monroe County, the site was chosen for the Genesee Country Village, a unique living history village form the nineteenth century. The village is home to approximately sixty-eight restored homes which individuals are able to explore while meeting guides from the past. In the village, though, there are three buildings which are a bit "para" normal in nature.

The Hyde House inside the Genesee Country Village is a unique octagon-shaped home originally from Friendship, New York. It was build by Corporal Hyde in 1870, shortly after the Civil War. Hyde was a farmer prior to the war but changed his career path after becoming involved with the nineteenth-century Spiritualism movement. He became schooled as a Homeopathic physician while his wife, Julia, was already an accomplished musician, but who would also become an ordained Spiritualist minister. It was common during these times to conduct séances in homes to communicate with long-passed spirits, and the Hyde Home was one of these homes. There were rumors that séances were a regular occurrence in the parlor. When Julia died, within two days of her husband, the

The porch of the Hyde House.
Photograph by Julie Fischer, Western New York Paranormal.

belief began to spread about their departed spirits frequently visiting the home. (Allegheny County, 2005)

In 1978, the Genesee Country Village acquired the Hyde House and moved it to their museum. Since its move, people have reported smelling the scent of flowers inside the building when there was no reasonable explanation for it. The sound of a piano key has also been heard. In an effort to calm rumors of the ghostly presence, Western New York Paranormal was asked to conduct a non-biased scientific investigation of the home in October of 2004. During the investigation, they stationed infrared video cameras throughout the building as well as lead investigators armed only with audio recorders and cameras. At the conclusion of the investigation, there were two pieces of material that were captured that could not be explained. A single photograph of a man wearing a fedora hat with the words "he caught me" on an audio recorder. Both taken just moments between each other. (An image of the man wearing the fedora hat is available by visiting the gallery section for Haunted Rochester at www.wnyparanormal.org.)

Another home of particular interest in the village is the Frank E. Davis Opera House. The opera house is said to have an energy all its own. Some people have claimed to hear the sound of applause from performances long past.

It was back in the 1980s when one of the re-enactors that was working in the Hamilton House in the village happened across another actor...or at least that is what he had thought. He stood at the top of one of the stairwells waiting for the next tour group to walk through when a woman wearing a Victorian-era dress turned the corner and began to walk up the stairs. As the gentleman turned to speak with her, she vanished into thin air.

The Genesee Country Village takes no official stance on the paranormal activity within their buildings or grounds nor does this author. The best advice on a trip to the Genesee Country Village is to go and enjoy this unique blend of living history. Just be mindful of the people you see walking around in era dress— are they truly re-enactors or spirits lost between worlds.

Big Springs Museum
3095 Main Street
Caledonia, New York

Once the local school of Caledonia, this three-story structure was converted in the early 1950s into a museum of local history. Individuals will discover on a tour through the museum artifacts that made the Caledonia region successful from areas of industry to agriculture.

While doing construction in the building, contractors were doing repairs in the building's main hall. They stepped out briefly for lunch locking the doors behind them, returning to find their power saw all bent and mangled. It was shortly after that they began to hear footsteps and see moving shadows in the building—when it was empty, except for those few people doing repairs.

During part of the renovations, a doorway was discovered on the third floor that was opened. It uncovered a small schoolroom. Today, it can be seen set up as a one-room school room with a teacher's desk at the front and a number of small desks lined up. What made this room unusual was that when it was uncovered, there was handwriting on a desk there which simply said, "ghosts are here." Perhaps a childish prank from a time long forgotten—or maybe a message from beyond? When this doorway opened, individuals with sensitivities who would walk through the building began to sense a strong, controlling energy. Some felt that it was one of a past teacher; a strict teacher. Children's laughter began to be heard along with more running footsteps, this time lighter, softer—definitely not those of an adult.

It's not uncommon for spiritual activity to increase in times of construction and change. The energy flow within a building changes, stirring the spirits. This may occur because they are uncomfortable with the change and sometimes it occurs because they have just been awakened after a long slumber. In this case, the dormant energy was awakened. Several spirits in fact. Museums will often gain attention from spirits who never resided inside the building itself. Many times, these souls will have attachments to objects that are brought in and then they begin to consider where they are currently in their new home. These spirits can either be residual energy that have no awareness of their surroundings or intelligent entities that begin to interact with those around them.

An investigation in 2006 of the building brought forth some very interesting results. Often on an investigation, researchers will have no physical interaction or actual real-time acknowledgement of spiritual activity. On this investigation, the researchers from Western New York Paranormal were on the third floor in a room that contained a large amount of artifacts from the World War II era. Researchers believe that for spirits to manifest, they need to pull energy from the environment around them.

When recording Electronic Voice Phenomenon, often a room will be flooded with white noise prior to attempting audio recordings. White noise is a sound generated on a single frequency that sounds much like static. It's believed that noise such as this can be used by entities, thereby making it easier for them to produce an audible response.

The researchers attempted to charge the room in a different manner, by using a strobe light at a controlled frequency. The premise they had was to use light to charge the room so that an entity might better manifest themselves in a photograph. As they allowed the light to "charge" the room, the researchers began asking questions, attempting to record Electronic Voice Phenomenon. However, as they asked questions, the responses came in a much different manner. The strobe light they were using began to change how it blinked. The light would become steady and flash in rhythm. The team asked the entity to blink the light once for *yes* and twice for *no*. They then asked, "Are you using the light to communicate?" The light blinked once. They then asked, "Are you happy we are here?" It blinked once again. Of course they had to ask if they were bothering the spirit and the response came back as two blinks. *No.* Over forty-five minutes this interchange occurred, with the investigators asking various questions about the entity, the museum, and some of the objects surrounding them. Each question tested the fact that the light was blinking and whether it was a true communication or not. Based on the responses received, the team felt this was a true communication.

In the small school room, the team had set up another experiment. They had placed a pendulum into a vacuum sealed jar. Pendulums are a common method of spiritual dowsing; they provide the spirit with a tool to respond to a researcher's questions. Under normal circumstances, an investigator would hold the pendulum suspended in one hand while asking questions. The pendulum would then sway back and forth or move in a circular pattern responding to *yes* or *no* questions. There is always a slight question as to the influence that the researcher has even on a sub-conscious level with a pendulum; therefore, in this case, the human element of the study was removed by sealing the pendulum in the jar and placing it on a desk. As the researchers watched and video recorded, they began to ask very simple yes or no questions of the entity. The pendulum began to quiver on its own with no outside interaction. No one moved about the room. The table was untouched and no vibrations were noted. Soon the pendulum began to respond to questions with very small movements, fluctuating back and forth. Another unexplained phenomenon had just occurred.

While in the small school room, psychic investigator Sarah Claud began to pick up the spirit of a young child. She sensed that he was between the ages of eight and ten. He had blond hair and was wearing a white t-shirt and overalls. The spirit was attached to an object on main floor and he now considered this place his home. He communicated to her that often he would run through the building playing hide and seek—even hiding objects at times. What made this interchange truly interesting was that, at the completion of the investigation, a photograph was shown to the investigators. It was a black and white photograph taken of the front of the building in 1976 during preparation for the centennial celebration. There, standing in front of the main doors, was a child around eight or ten years old with blond hair and overalls. It was the same boy Claud had spoken with in spirit. The museum member explained that the child had not been present when the photograph was taken. No one was wearing circa-era clothing that day. They couldn't explain it.

Valentown Ghost Town
7373 Valentown Square
Victor, New York
www.valentown.org

Originally built in 1879, Levi Valentine built this one-building town. Within the four-story building was housed every retail establishment that most nineteenth-century towns had, including a general store and blacksmith's shop. It even had a grand ball room for community functions. At the time Valentown was built, it was the intention that the railroads would arrive and invigorate the town. However, the railroad never reached Valentown, and eventually, the building was vacated and left untouched. In 1940, the building was purchased by Sheldon Fisher and it was renovated into a museum.

Several ghost hunting organizations have investigated Valentown with the intention of documenting the claims of spiritual activity in the building. Some of the phenomenon reported to occur are footsteps and voices coming from locked rooms, pages of a magazine turning by themselves from within a glass display case, suitcases moving by themselves, and a shadowy figure passing right through a closed door. There is also the spontaneous tinkling of the old-fashioned bell hanging on the door to the General Store and the intermittent beeping of the building's security sensor. Neighbors have also reported a white shadowy presence in their home and that of a man dressed in period clothing which appears in both the front and rear windows of the building, depending on whether one is coming or going, oil lanterns swaying, lights turning themselves on and off, and even the sound of music.

In November of 2006, the Atlantic Paranormal Association (TAPS) brought the film crew from the Sci-Fi channel to the location for an episode of *Ghost Hunters*. The investigators set up their equipment for a weekend-long investigation of the building. Film crews and investigators swarmed all over the entire building throughout the weekend recording and documenting. One of the lead investigators told Carol Finch, President of the Historical Society, that he had witnessed an unexplained shadow figure on the second floor near the generator room. Unfortunately, he was not able to catch any scientific evidence of it. There were many other personal experiences that weekend, including muted music, unexplained voices, and other sounds, as well as floating orbs. Regrettably, when the team wrapped up their investigation, they lost all of their data. Perhaps a spiritual prankster at work?

Since then, many other groups have investigated the building some with interesting results, and others obtaining nothing. Sometimes an individual can go into a location that is just overridden with ghosts, but if said ghosts don't want to make their presences known, they simply won't.

The investigators from Flower City Paranormal have made several visits to Valentown, always picking up something they just can't explain. Some of the things experienced were footsteps, sounds of a music box, shadowy figures, and Electronic Voice Phenomenon.

Some of the most interesting evidence captured at the Valentown site was by Western New York Paranormal. In an investigation conducted shortly after TAPS had filmed their episode, the group set up a variety of surveillance cameras throughout the building while combing the area with their investigators. In the top-floor ballroom, a photograph was captured of a shadowy figure. Although features were not able to be identified, the individual looked like a female wearing a black mourning dress. Could this be one of the figures that visitors have noticed in the building? An image of the shadow woman can be seen by visiting the gallery section for Haunted Rochester at www.wnyparanormal.org. Here is where you will also be able to see a video clip of the moving apparition that was captured there

It was on the second floor, in an area that had been set up as a blacksmith's shop, that the most convincing evidence of life after death was captured. The cameras of the Western New York Paranormal team captured a full-bodied ghostly apparition walking with a limping gait down a pathway and off the screen of their night-vision video camera, which had been placed in the room at the beginning of their investigation. The spirit had been noted by one of the psychic investigators earlier in the evening as a male spirit with a severe limp. When watching the video, the figure appears first as a solid form, then

Even among the old stables, the spirits still linger.

An unexplained object captured in several photographs inside and outside the building. The camera was taken in for a tune-up afterwards, finding no mechanical dysfunction. *Photography by Dorothy Goodno, Western New York Paranormal.*

becomes transparent, wandering aimlessly along its path and away from the camera's eye.

What made this night so different than all the rest for the team? Why would this group pick up evidence such as this? It was a once-in-a-lifetime find. Could it have been caused by the fierce electric storm raging outside that night? Perhaps the electrical charge of the storm gave the entity more power to manifest. Regardless of reason, the finding boggled the investigators and skeptics alike.

Two years later, Monroe County Paranormal Investigations visited Valentown. Their psychic investigator came across this entity himself. The spirit had a message: "Tell Dwayne he was lucky on the 21st." No one but the team of Western New York Paranormal could make the psychic connection: The date stamp on their digital recorder was wrong by two days. The investigation they had performed was on the 21st.

In the fall of 2008, amateur paranormal investigator Jessica Smith brought her small team of investigators to the legendary building in Victor. They had heard all of the rumors and reports

Notice in the upper left hand of the photograph the skull. Below it is an enlarged copy of this grim reaper. *Photograph by Jamie Smith of Rochester, New York*

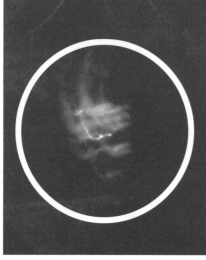

Above: Close up of the previous photograph. Note: the upper left hand of the photograph, the skull has been circled. Below it is an enlarged copy of this grim reaper.

Left: Detail.

of hauntings surrounding the building—but instead decided to concentrate their investigative efforts in the woods nearby the building. The feelings of being watched and followed were very apparent, especially in an area near an old water well. It was when they began to take pictures that they began to capture mists among them with mysterious streams of light—but perhaps the most shocking was the face that they captured peering at them from the darkness—the face of a grim reaper.

Genesee County Historical Society
3 West Main Street
Batavia, New York
www.co.genesee.ny.us/dpt/countyclerk/historians.html

A short, thirty-minute drive from the city of Rochester, Batavia offers some interesting adventures for the paranormal explorer. The Genesee County Historical Society is one of the best places to start your search for the unknown. They have a wealth of knowledge about the region, which has become affectionately known as the "Supernatural Genesee." There are tales of spooks and ghosts galore in this area, some of which begin right inside the Historical Society itself.

The building in which the Historical Society resides is perhaps one of the most unique and breath-taking in the city of Batavia. The large brick building they occupy was built in 1824, which housed the original Batavia Fire Department. There have been documented events that have occurred through the past 100 years at the old engine house in Batavia. The building has been home to many things including a mill, fire station, and most recently county maintenance and the Historical Society. Ex-employees and visitors have experienced physical touches, smells, and have shared reports of seeing fully-formed apparitions.

One past employee tells of a night she was working late in the historical department. The building was empty with the exception of herself. As she worked, she began to hear noises from the main lobby area. Thinking nothing of it, she continued to work until the noises became louder. It sounded like the sounds of someone one floor above the lobby. As she walked out into the lobby area, she noted that she didn't see anyone. Well, that was nothing until she looked up to the balcony overlooking the main lobby area! There she saw a man dressed all in black. She reached over to turn the lights on, believing it to be another employee who had sneaked into the building, but as she did, the figure disappeared into thin air and was gone.

The county historian, Susan Conklin, tells of one night that she was working at her desk only to have someone tap her on the shoulder. Turning to see who needed her, she found no one there. As she went back to work, she began to notice shadows moving at the side of her vision. Then a smell began to build; it was the smell of smoke—sulfury, sooty smoke from a fire. The scent was followed by the sound of a gasping breath and cough.

Some believe that the building holds the spirit of a long-past fire fighter as well as others, including the soul of a mill worker who died in a fire a hundred years ago. There really isn't a concrete answer to the presence that remains at the old engine house, but according to paranormal investigators from Western New York Paranormal, there are definitely some spirits still walking the halls. On the upper floor balcony, they captured a very distinct EVP of a male asking for "help." In a locker room area that is not normally available to the public, they witnessed a door opening itself and captured it on video tape.

12

HALLS
OF PARANORMAL LEARNING

Halls of greater learning have been subject to stories of the paranormal for decades. Urban legend and myth lead many schools to have similar stories. There are few universities that a lack of a story of a college student dying in a dorm or of a spectre who wanders the campus endlessly, looking for lost souls. There are some stories that bear the fruit of truth—stories that have historical backing and step beyond the harmless fraternity prank and into the unknown world of the paranormal.

University of Rochester
Rush Rhees Library
Rochester, New York
www.rit.edu

Part of any college student's life involves a tremendous amount of study-time in the library. One of the most beautiful libraries on the University of Rochester Campus is the Rush Rhees Library. Built in the late 1920s, it is a pillar of elegance and beauty. Unfortunately, however, within the building, a young construction worker died as a result of an accidental fall. His name was Pete Nicosia, a young Sicilian mason worker who had recently come to America.

Though Nicosia died over eighty years ago, his spirit is still remembered in these hallowed halls. In fact, students who work late hours in the Rush Rhees Library at the University of Rochester sometimes catch more than a glimpse into academia. It's been said that sometimes, late at night, a figure of a man in his late 40s has been seen walking among the bookshelves. Now, not many would think much of this. It's a college campus with thousands of students who are night owls. The difference is that this gentleman is wearing the clothes of a construction worker from the 1930s. Some students have even spoken with him, not realizing he was only a spectre.

University of Rochester
Tierman Hall
Rochester, New York

Western New York winters are regarded as some of the harshest in the northeast. There can be plenty of snow and plummeting temperatures, making a small pond next to one of the dorms at the campus of the University of Rochester beautiful during the winter. This small pond is full of folklore and has had many spiritual sightings over the past forty years.

It was back in the 1960s when two students accidentally fell through the ice on the pond. They had walked off into the woods for a romantic stroll together, when suddenly a terrible mistake occurred—they'd accidentally walked out onto the icy pond, and the ice gave way. It wasn't until the next day that their friends noticed they were missing, and a search began in earnest across the campus. One rescue worker found the broken hole in the ice and immediately a search of the pond began. They were both found shortly afterwards under the ice.

Since then, students have shared stories of seeing two people walking on the ice on cold winter evenings, and then vanishing into thin air.

State University of New York at Brockport
Brockport, New York
www.brockport.edu

The city of Brockport is just thirty minutes west of Rochester. Like the city of Rochester, it was built as a canal town. Originally known as Brockway's Port, the initial settlement began in 1802. The area quickly grew in its first decade, becoming a home to 683 settlers, its industry growing as a result of the canal. Today, Brockport is home to more than 8,000 people and it continues to grow.

It was in 1841 that the village of Brockport expanded its horizons, and complete construction of Brockport made tremendous strides with the construction of the Brockport Collegiate Institute in 1841—which would later became the Brockport State Normal School in 1866. The term "normal" refers to the fact that the school could only offer certification programs as opposed to degree programs. It was in 1948, when the school became known as the Brockport State Teacher's College, that it fell under the newly formed SUNY education system.

Today SUNY Brockport has more than 8,700 students attending its halls, easily doubling the population of the village. But as with most colleges, there is also a lesser-known population on campus—a paranormal population. SUNY Brockport is no different than other schools around the country: ripe with local legend and lore. Most of its stories and reports center around Harter Hall, the original collegiate institute and oldest building on campus. There have been reports from the cleaning staff over the years of hearing people roaming among the hallways, talking, as well as doors opening and closing with no one else in the building.

According to a report in the local campus paper, one member of the janitorial staff was standing on a ladder, changing a light bulb in one of the halls, when she felt her leg grabbed. Startled, she turned to find no one there and slipped off the ladder. She found herself caught by a gentle, unseen force that rested her on the floor safely. Other reports often come from the basement of Harter Hall. Still heard are the sounds of water splashing and people laughing from the pool that was once there.

One other account of paranormal activity is from a suite at Mortimer Hall. Mortimer Hall is one of the older dorm complexes on the campus. The suite is said to be the home of a spirit who committed suicide there in the 1970s. A brief examination of this story seems to support the suicide claim. Girls staying inside the suite claim to have had personal items disappear, reappearing shortly thereafter in different locations. These personal effects weren't moved by the girls. One of the students woke up one night to a bright light hovering above her bed. She says it hovered there for a short period of time, then moved to a corner and disappeared, as she called her boyfriend in fear. Lights in the suite are said to turn themselves on spontaneously in the middle of the night.

Of course, ghostly experiences often happen when individuals least expect them. So many times when paranormal investigation teams go in to evaluate potential unexplained phenomenon in a location, they come up empty handed. Just as in life, when we ask someone to perform a "trick," it is still up to that individual whether or not they comply. This wasn't the case, though, of a paranormal investigation conducted at SUNY Brockport by Long Island Paranormal Investigators. During their investigation they experienced lights turning on and off by themselves several times throughout the night. Upon further examination, it was noted that the lights were not motion-sensitive and there was no one else in the area who could have turned them on.

13

PARANORMAL TERMS

A Glossary

Angel
A benevolent spirit who has never lived that watches over and is a servant of God.

Anomaly
This refers to anything that is out of place or unexplained. For instance, flare from a camera flash in a mirror is not an anomaly. There is a reason that it appears in the photograph. A mist or vapor that takes on the form of a person is an anomaly.

Apparition
The word apparition was used as far back as the seventeenth century in reference to any type of spirit that has the appearance of a solid, physical state.

Automatic writing
When a spirit takes over the arm and hand of a medium to communicate through writing a message using a pen and paper.

Cleansing

The use of prayer or other ritual to remove negative or unwanted energies from a location.

Dead of Night

Also known as the witching hour, the time is not midnight, but actually around 3 am. This is the time when the veil is thinnest between realms and dark entities are at their strongest power. In many ways, it is a mockery of the trinity and an exact opposite time of when Christ died on the cross.

Demon

An evil spirit that has never lived. More powerful than man with unlimited knowledge and power, but still governed by God's rules. In the army of Satan, demons are the grunts of the army.

Devils

An evil spirit more powerful than the demonic. They have never lived and have no soul. They are more powerful than the demonic and can be viewed, in a manner of speaking, as the commanding officers.

Dowsing

The art of using a pendulum or set of brass or copper rods to communicate with spirit.

EMF (Electromagnetic Field)

It is believed that all life forms have energy. When they die, the energy has to go someplace, according to the laws of physics, therefore, it is released into the environment. Some believe this to be the soul or consciousness of the individual. Scientific studies have been conducted measuring electrical energy and body mass at the time of death. When death occurs, there is a slight body mass loss and an electrical discharge. It is believed that in order for spirits to manifest, they must gather additional energy, causing changes in the electromagnetic field (magnetic and electrical). These variations can be measured by special meters such as tri-field meters, elf meters and even compasses.

Entity
A ghost.

EVP (Electronic Voice Phenomenon)
The capture of ghost voices on recorded media. These voices will not be heard at the time of recording but will be heard upon its playback. These are usually simple, one-word responses or short phrases, recorded well above or below the range of human hearing.

Fox Sisters
Sisters Kate, Leah, and Margaret Fox played an important role in the creation of the Spiritualism religious movement by utilizing spirit communication.

Ghost
A spirit who lingers in this world or travels between realms.

Ghost Hunt
An attempt made by the living to find, see, or document a ghost or spirit.

Ghost Hunter
A living individual who searches out and sometime finds or identifies ghosts and spirits.

Gray Lady
The ghost of a woman who has died at the hands of a lover or waits for the return of a loved one.

Haunt
A place to which a ghost, or ghosts, frequently return.

Haunting
The continuous manifestation of inexplicable phenomena associated with the presence of ghosts or spirits attached to a particular location.

Haunted
An object, location, or person who receives visitations from departed spirits.

Leylines
Energy pathways through the earth that can act as conduits of spiritual energy.

Medium
An individual who communicates with spirits.

Mist
A vaporous substance that appears in photographs and is believed to be the spirit beginning to manifest.

Night Shot
Some video and still cameras have the ability to operate with near 0 lux, utilizing a special feature that uses infrared lighting.

Orb
A spherical ball of light often thought to be spirit energy that commonly appears in photographs in areas that have paranormal activity. Orbs are often captured in photographs and video but sometimes can be seen with the naked eye. Since spherical shapes are the easiest and most coherent shapes to form, it is believed that the spirit orb is the most fundamental of the spirit levels. There is much controversy as to whether orbs actually exist or whether they are simply particles of moisture or dust. Many paranormal groups define true spiritual orbs as those that emit their own light, show evidence of movement, and, upon closer examination, have a structural component to them demonstrating a nucleic look inside the orb itself.

Occult
This refers to studies of the magical or mystical.

Ouija®
A divination tool that allows individuals to speak with spirits. The original Ouija® boards were simply a wine glass tipped upside down with scrabble pieces placed on a table. Individuals would touch the rim of the glass and ask questions of the spirits. The glass would then slide from letter to letter spelling out the response. Parker Brothers later made this game popular and it is still manufactured in Salem, Massachusetts, today. Many believe that Ouija® boards are gateways to the demonic, while others believe it to be the intention placed behind it.

Pagan
A follower of nature-based religion. Pagan comes from the Latin "Paganus," meaning "Country Dweller." Pagan is a term used to describe Shamans, Druids, Wiccans, Heathens, and other polytheistic religions.

Paranormal
Refers to something operating outside the boundaries of explanation.

Paranormal Investigator
An individual who conducts scientific research of unexplained phenomenon.

Pendulum
A small weight at the end of a string or chain used for divination.

Phantom Hitchhiker or Traveler
A ghost or spirit that haunts a particular stretch of road or route. Phantom hitchhikers ask for rides, only to suddenly disappear when they reach their destination.

Photographic Apparitions
Ghosts and spirits that you can't see, yet appear on photographs after they are developed.

Poltergeist
From the German meaning "noisy ghost," this term has been in use since the early nineteenth century to mean a spirit that makes noise, or otherwise plays pranks—often annoying ones. Unlike other ghosts, poltergeists can move from one location to another, following the person they've chosen to torment.

Portal
An entry point into our world from that of the spiritual realm. Mirrors are common portal points and have been used for centuries by magicians to scry or communicate with spirit.

Protection
Spiritual ritual, such as prayer, which guards individuals from spiritual attack.

Psychic
An individual who receives impressions from the environment and feels energy. They commonly are able to sense energy and its movements.

Residual energy
Energy that is left behind after a traumatic or powerful event. This is common in areas such as battlefields where much tragedy has occurred. Individuals may sense a deep sluggish feeling or, while in areas such inside an old theater, may feel the powerful positive energy of an excited crowd.

Residual haunting
A haunting that repeats itself over and over again like an old film. Generally, these are caused by a traumatic event.

Séance
The gathering of a group of individuals for the purpose of communicating to the ghosts of the dead.

Sensitive
Someone who is aware of, or can detect, paranormal events beyond the range of their five human senses.

Spirit
The soul of a human being.

Spiritualism
Formed as a religion in the nineteenth century by the Fox Sisters, it is based on the belief system that ghosts and spirits can, and do, communicate with the living.

Supernatural
Something that exists or occurs through some means other than a known force in nature or science.

Toning
The practice of using vocalization on specific frequencies to cleanse a home of negative energy.

Walkers
Dark shadow figures that appear mainly in cemeteries wandering the grounds. They are residual in nature and do not acknowledge an investigator's presence.

Wiccan
An individual who follows the religion of Wicca. Wicca is a nature-based religion based on pre-Christian beliefs that honors the earth as sacred and sees deities as both male and female, God and Goddess. Wicca was founded by Gerald Gardner in the 1950s.

Witching Hour

Also known as the dead of night, occurring at about 3 am (and is not the midnight hour as commonly thought). This is the time when the veil is thinnest between realms, and dark entities are at their strongest power. In many ways, it is a mockery of the trinity and an exact opposite time of when Christ died on the cross.

White Noise

A sound generated on a single frequency that sounds much like static. It's believed that noise such as this can be used by entities, making it easier for them to produce an audible response.

14

ROCHESTER'S
PARANORMAL RESEARCHERS

T here are several paranormal research teams that work in the Rochester, New York, region. These individuals are an excellent resource for anyone interested in the haunting of the region.

Flower City Paranormal

Founded by Stephanie Giglio and Lindsay Helett, this group takes a very skeptical look into paranormal investigation in the Rochester region. www.flowercityparanormal.com.

Phantom Finders

Monroe County Phantom Finders was formed in May 2007 with only three members. Today, there are more than 130, with a very active core group. Regular monthly meetings are very well attended. A specific topic for discussion is set for each meeting and then opened for general discussion and socialization. They schedule two outside ghost hunts a month during the summer and one inside hunt a month during winter. Overnight events and day trip events frequently occur. They feel there is a need for this type of group in the Monroe County area and welcome new members to enjoy their hunts, which are always successful and enjoyable. They also offer successful home cleansing, for those "pesky ghosties" that seem to get into homes and annoy the occupants. However, they make it a practice to never deal with negative forces or demonic forces, preferring to work with spirits of a more benign nature. www.paranormal.meetup. com/464.

Monroe County Paranormal Investigations

The team is lead by paranormal researchers Rob and Kat Pistilli of Rochester, New York. Their investigative team researches the paranormal using a combination of science and spiritualism that they have developed over several years of investigation. www.monroeghosts.com.

Mystic Encounters

A paranormal research team that presents their local Rochester findings on Fairport's local cable access television. www.mysticencounters.org.

RE Paranormal

Lead by professional photographer Ralph Esposito, his group conducts a variety of investigations of private residences and public areas. www.reparanormal.com.

Rochester Paranormal

An organization formed in 1982 by Director Joseph Burkart, this paranormal organization provides research on spiritual hauntings, cryptozoology, and unidentified flying objects, among other unexplained phenomena in the Rochester, New York area. www.rochesterparanormal.com.

Rochester Paranormal Society

Formed in 2002, a group of investigators who have come together to discover the truth about what is out there. www.myspace.com/flerbyherby.

Rochester Investigators into the Paranormal (RIP)

A group of young investigators whose goal is to simply collect evidence of paranormal activity. Their Web site serves as a resource where their carefully-evaluated findings are displayed. The evidence comes from their members, who venture in from all walks of life, bringing their personal experiences with the paranormal, which provides an interesting outlook on the phenomenon they have captured. www.freewebs.com/ripny/.

Rolling Hills Paranormal Research Society

A paranormal research group dedicated to investigating the paranormal phenomenon of the old Genesee County Nursing Home/Asylum approximately an hour South of Rochester, New York. www.rhprs.com.

Trippi Paranormal

A paranormal research team based out of Fairport, New York, that researches and explores unexplained paranormal activity. Their investigations are scientifically based. www.trippiparanormal.com.

Wayne Area Ghost Society

This group was founded in 2006 by Wayne County, New York, residents Tom and Becky Sawtelle. They are a group of amateur paranormal investigators who focus on purported haunting (they don't chase UFOs). wayneareaghosts.webs.com/.

Western New York Paranormal of Rochester and Buffalo

Western New York Paranormal is recognized as a 501c(3) non-profit corporation by New York State and the Internal Revenue Service. The group was formed as a resource for Western New York that would provide educational and investigative services for suspected paranormal activity limited to reports of ghosts, hauntings, poltergeist, and life after death encounters. Special emphasis is placed on darker demonic hauntings. www.wnyparanormal.org.

Wyoming County Investigators into the Paranormal

These individuals have helped many by discovering the truth, aiding homeowners in connecting them with loved ones who have passed on, and by proving or disproving the haunting of a home. www.wciotp.com.

15

HAUNTED TOURISM
Ghost Walks

Chilling Tales From Rochester's Past
This ever popular Halloween program runs every October. Lantern-bearing guides lead participants under the cloak of darkness through the streets as they hear bone-chilling real stories from Rochester's past, with actors bringing the stories to life. www.landmarksociety.org.

Rochester Candlelight Ghost walks
Halloween ghost walks are made available to the public in Charlotte and in the area of the Mt. Hope Cemetery. These walks share the history and ghost stories of the area, while allowing you to communicate with the spirits along the way, utilizing diving rods and other methods. www.rochestercandlelightghostwalks.com.

Rolling Hills Ghost Hunts
Once a poor house. Once an insane asylum. Once a nursing home. Once a country mall. Now a paranormal research center,

Rolling Hills Ghost hunts allows individuals to explore four floors, more than 100 rooms, and underground tunnels in search of paranormal phenomenon. Ghost and historical tours are available. www.rollinghills-ghosthunts.com.

Valentown Ghost Hunts

Public ghost hunting opportunities are offered Friday and Saturday evenings, and also during the week by special arrangement. Roam the halls of Valentown with your own cameras and audio recorders in search of the unknown. www.valentown.org.

AFTERWORDS

I t is my hope that this book will inspire a new age of paranormal explorers. It will take all of us to find the answers, no matter who we are or the background from which we come. I hope that you will boldly explore, with passion and respect, the haunted places that has been presented here sharing your finding and stories with others.

In the future, as Rochester grows and is explored more deeply, there will be an update of the Ghost Hunter's Guide. You see, everyone has a ghost story to tell and the surface has only been scratched with this first book—who knows how many other stories of spectres and phantoms lie in the buried history of Rochester? If you have any stories you'd like to share, feedback you'd like to share, or suggestions for future book updates, please send them to:

Dwayne Claud
Western New York Paranormal
Web site: www.wnyparanormal.org
E-mail: wnyparanormal@aol.com

BIBLIOGRAPHY

_____. "A spirited halloween." *Democrat and Chronicle*. October 31, 1993.

_____. "Bodies of twins found in cemetery." *Democrat and Chronicle*. May 29, 1908.

_____. "Scary trip to the dentist." 13WHAM. September 21, 2006.

Barone, Donald. "Seeking some baseball spirit." Broadcast Report. ESPN. 2005.

Borick, Anna. "The haunting of Rolling Hills." [online] Available. *Ghost! Magazine*. www.ghostmag.com/archive-rolling_hills.htm 2007.

_____. "Gothic Street House." Personal Interview. May 22, 2008.

_____. "Spirits guided him to build 3,000 miles of railroad track." *New York Times*. June 15, 1922.

_____. Private Interview. "University of Rochester." May 12, 2007.

_____. Various cases. [online] Available www.wnyparanormal. com.

Allegany County Web site. "The Hyde house." [online]. www.usgennet.org/usa/ny/county/allegany/FriendshipOctagonHome/FriendshipOctagon.htm 2005.

Baker, Thomas. "Old Jim." Personal Interview. July 22, 2008.

Bryant, Erica. "Really Rochester. Powers Building Beautiful Spooky." [online] Available. *Rochester Insider*. www.rochesterinsider.com/outside/20040319out743.shtml, 2006.

Claud, Sarah. Personal Interview. July 24, 2008.

Conklin, Sue. Personal Interview. "Genesee County Museum" and "Rolling Hills." September 2006.

Dorson, Richard M. "The wonderful leaps of Sam Patch." [online] Available. *American Heritage Magazine.* www.americanheritage.com/articles/magazine/ah/1966/1/1966_1_12.shtml, January 1, 1966.

Daughtery, Carole. "The Apparition on Stryker Road." *Democrat and Chronicle.* October 27, 2007.

Edmiston, Jennifer. Personal Interview. November 2006.

Esposito, Ralph, RE Paranormal and Rochester Candlelite Ghostwalks. Personal Interview. March 2007.

Esposito, Ralph. "Green Lantern Inn" DVD. *Mystic Encounters* 2007.

Keene, Micheal. "Farmers Tavern and Inn" and "Fox Sisters." Personal Interview. March 11, 2008.

O'Brien, Micheal. "Springbrook Inn" Broadcast News. *R-News Rochester,* October 31, 2006.

Oneski, Jenni. East Coast Paranormal and Rochester Candlelite Ghostwalks. Personal Interview. October 2005.

Randall, Bruce. Personal Interview. July 15, 2008.

Ryan, Tim. "Geva Theater." Personal interview. March 14, 2008.

Steinmetz, Lisa. Personal Interview. May 2007.

Wagner, Patricia. Personal Interview. April 27, 2008.

Wilson, Vince. Personal Interview. March 25, 2007.

Winfield, Mason. "Haunted Places of Western New York." *Western New York Wares.* 2003.

Yronwade, Catherine. "Hoodoo in theory and practice." [online] Available. www.luckymojo.com/hoodoo.html, 2008.

Zaccarai, Gary. "Auditorium Theatre." Personal Interview. May 12, 2008.

INDEX